REAL CITY

Rome

www.realcity.dk.com

LONDON, NEW YORK,
MELBOURNE, MUNICH AND DELHI
www.dk.com

Produced by Departure Lounge LLP

Contributors
Charlotte Eager, Sylvie Hogg, Jason Horowitz, Frances Kennedy,
Raffaella Malaguti, Sally Washington

Photographer
Alessandra Santarelli

Reproduced in Singapore by Colourscan
Printed and bound in Singapore by Tien Wah Press

First published in Great Britain in 2007
by Dorling Kindersley Limited
80 Strand, London WC2R 0RL

Previously published as Rome eGuide, 2005

A CIP catalogue record is available from the British Library.

ISBN: 978-1-40531-804-4

The information in this Real City guide is checked annually.

This guide is supported by a dedicated website which provides the very latest information for visitors
to Rome; please see page 7 for the web address and password. Some information, however, is
liable to change, and the publishers cannot accept responsibility for any consequences arising from
the use of this book, nor for any material on third party websites, and cannot guarantee that any
website address in this book will be a suitable source of travel information.
We value the views and suggestions of our readers very highly. Please write to:
Publisher, DK Eyewitness Travel Guides,
Dorling Kindersley, 80 Strand, London WC2R 0RL, Great Britain.

REAL CITY

Rome

Contents

The Guide

Real City Rome

Stay ahead of the crowd with **Real City Rome**, and find the best places to eat, shop, drink and chill out at a glance.

The guide is divided into four main sections:

Introducing Rome – essential background information on the city, including an overview by one of the authors, the top tourist attractions, festivals and seasonal events, and useful travel and practical information.

Listings – eight themed chapters packed with incisive reviews of the best the city has to offer, in every price band and chosen by local experts.

Street Finder – map references in the listings lead you to this section, where you can plan your route and find your way around.

Indexes – the By Area and By Type indexes offer shortcuts to what you are looking for, whether it is a bar in Trastevere or a seafood restaurant.

The Website

www.realcity.dk.com

By purchasing this book you have been granted free access to up-to-the-minute online content about Rome for at least 12 months. Click onto **www.realcity.dk.com** for updates, and sign up for a free weekly email with the latest information on what to see and do in Rome.

On the website you can:

- **Find the latest news** about Rome, including exhibitions, restaurant openings and music events

- Check what other readers have to say and **add your own comments** and reviews

- **Plan your visit** with a customizable calendar

- See at a glance **what's in and what's not**

- Look up listings by name, by type and by area, and check the **latest reviews**

- **Link directly** to all the websites in the book, and many more

How to register

> Click on the Rome icon on the home page of the website to register or log in.

> Enter the city code given on this page, and follow the instructions given.

> The city code will be valid for a minimum of 12 months from the date you purchased this guide.

city code: **rome10472**

introducing rome

When in Rome, do as the Romans do: indulge in a long lunch, hang out in a piazza watching the world go by, catch a gig or performance at a *centro sociale*, or grab a *gelato* and stroll under the stars. Our contributors have selected the best of what Rome has to offer and we open with an overview that sets the scene for a visit to this ancient and romantic city.

INTRODUCING ROME

Rome's pedigree is ancient, but there's nothing stuffy or exclusive about it. A sunny, youthful spirit pervades the Italian capital, and the marble-clad, ochre-washed city of emperors and popes is as alluring as ever. But Rome also has plenty of grit and rough edges that keep it real. From the relentless barrage of staggering art and architecture to the chaotic traffic and ebullient locals, Rome is a sublimely percussive place that will make your soul vibrate.

Sylvie Hogg

It's a Small Town, After All

Rome is the capital city of one of the eight most-industrialized nations in the world, but don't come here expecting a sophisticated, fast-paced metropolis – it's not Milan, whose focus on fashion and finance creates an altogether different urban environment. Rome is still a provincial town in many ways, which is one of the reasons we love it. In the late 19th century, Rome's population was barely 100,000, and farmers grazed their cattle in the Roman Forum; today, there are over three million people living in the city, and the Forum is preserved as a major archaeological site. Rome's relatively recent growth spurt is key to understanding the nature of its people. The typical born-and-bred *romano de' Roma* is old-fashioned, provincial, boisterous, even coarse, but with strong ties to community and family. No one is so rushed that they won't stop to get coffee with someone they recognize on the street; and if you're looking to meet someone for a drink you hardly need to make plans, as almost everyone converges at one of two *centro storico* piazzas for their *aperitivo* every night.

As in much of Italy, rules and laws are still relaxed in Rome: motorists can usually talk their way out a traffic ticket, and young women can easily persuade military police to escort them home from a distant club at 3am. Once you get past the outward mayhem and traffic, Rome is a lively and compact city whose people are warm and welcoming.

A Cinematic Stage, Filled with Stars

Visual splendour is inextricable from the identity of Rome, and the "spectacle" of Rome is much more than the still-life created by imposing monuments and artistic treasures. Those who inhabit the city today are well aware that they've inherited an extraordinary backdrop – of ruins, churches, fountains and obelisks set amid a dramatically rolling topography and lit by warm Mediterranean light – against which to play out their daily lives. Romans are always in character on their cinematic stage: in every piazza, impromptu pageants unfold before your eyes as locals shout and gesticulate about topics as mundane as groceries and drycleaning.

a city primer

While all the melodrama that Romans pump into their existence isn't strictly warranted, it is basic to *romanità*. And yes, they know they have an audience. In this spectacular city, few people are interested in going unnoticed.

A More Convincing Modern Energy

Apart from its film industry, Rome hasn't made headlines for its artistic or architectural output for several centuries. Change is under way, however. The presence of contemporary design and culture in Rome has grown from a faint tapping into a resounding beat in recent years. This modern energy is showing up in new hotels that have enlisted international design teams, and in a fresh crop of worldly restaurants, bars and boutiques that are a far cry from the provincial feel of the city's more traditional eating, drinking, and shopping establishments. Having known only classical monuments and red-check tablecloth trattorias for such a long time, Romans are relishing the change in the scenery. A slew of brand-new cultural spaces – the Auditorium performing arts centre, the MAXXI museum

for 21st-century art, the Casa del Jazz – have been enormously well-received by locals and have impressed international critics. But Rome has also incorporated the old into some of the new, brilliantly converting defunct slaughterhouses, power stations, and papal stables into exhibition halls with an avant-garde edge. Though it's not likely that the wood-shelved *enoteca* will ever go out of style, Rome's hottest bars and lounges are more design-conscious than ever, providing a bit of the cosmopolitan playground that Romans had only ever seen in cities such as New York and London. But don't expect too much of a sweeping revolution: Rome's character is still deeply rooted in its lengthy history, and any transformation is bound to be gradual.

✅ The Good Value Mark

Cities can be expensive, but if you know where to go you can always discover excellent-value places. We've picked out the best of these in the Restaurants, Shopping, and Hotels chapters and indicated them with the pink Good Value mark.

INTRODUCING ROME

A stroll through Rome's historical centre takes you past
some of the world's most stunning monuments and most
celebrated museums. At every turn, the city bombards you
with dramatic Baroque squares and fountains and enduring
ancient remains. The best-known sights are not where
you'll find the soul of modern Rome, but the breathtaking
splendour and rich history of these places are difficult to
resist on any visit to the Eternal City.

Colosseum

`9 F1`

Piazza del Colosseo • 06 3996 7700 • Ⓜ Colosseo
Open 9am–1hr before sunset daily

Gladiators and wild animals fought to the death within the *Amphi-theatrum Flavium* every other day at the height of the Roman Empire.
Even if you simply stare at it from the street, the Colosseum inspires
awe for bygone ancient glory like no other monument in Rome. **Adm**

Roman Forum

`9 E1`

Entrances on Via Sacra, Largo Romolo e Remo, Via del Foro Romano
06 3996 7700 • Ⓜ Colosseo Open 9am–1hr before sunset daily

This valley of solitary arches and fragmentary columns was the meet-ing place of ancient Rome and the centre of the civilized world for
almost 1,000 years. The ruins are romantic but confusing: a guide is
essential to make sense of the temples and other sites *(see p89)*.

St Peter's Basilica

`1 B3`

Piazza San Pietro, Vatican City • 06 6988 4466 • Ⓜ Cipro Musei Vaticani
Open 7am–7pm daily

Bernini's elliptical piazza is a grand embrace, and Michelangelo's
dome crowns the skyline, but the interior of St Peter's is most
impressive. The vast Vatican basilica, completed in 1626, is a huge
treasure chest of artistic masterpieces – including Michelangelo's
Pietà – and it's all clad in marble, bronze and gold *(see p94)*.

For the very latest on Rome go to ≫ **www.realcity.dk.com**

top attractions

Pantheon 7 E2

Piazza della Rotonda • 06 6830 0230 • Bus Nos. 40 Express, 62, 87, 492
Open 8:30am–7:30pm Mon–Sat, 9am–6pm Sun

The 2nd-century AD "temple of all gods" is the best-preserved example of Roman architecture and engineering genius. A vast concrete dome, pierced by an opening that lets in light and rain, is suspended over a round chamber faced with polychrome marble from Africa *(see p77)*.

Galleria Borghese 3 F5

Villa Borghese • 06 32 810 • Bus Nos. 52, 53, 11, 910
≫ **www.galleriaborghese.it** Open 9am–7pm Tue–Sun (booking essential)

A mix of Roman mosaics and statuary, Renaissance painting and Baroque sculpture makes this one of the world's best art galleries. Bernini's astonishing marbles are the museum's uncontested stars, but Caravaggio's and Titian's works also shine *(see p84)*. **Adm**

Vatican Museums and Sistine Chapel 1 B3

Viale Vaticano, Vatican City • 06 6988 3333 • Ⓜ Cipro Musei Vaticani
≫ **mv.vatican.va** Open 8:45–4:45 Mon–Fri, 8:45–1:45 Sat & last Sun of the month (Nov–Feb: 8:45–1:45 Mon–Sat). Closed Catholic holidays; check website for details

During the 1500s, the popes began hoarding the Greek and Roman sculpture that is the core of the collection in these mile-long galleries. They also commissioned Raphael and Michelangelo to fresco their private apartments and the famed Sistine Chapel *(see p94)*. **Adm**

≫ *From Apr–Oct, avoid the morning crowds at the Vatican Museums by visiting after lunch Mon–Fri*

INTRODUCING ROME

Piazza Navona

6 D2

Bus Nos. 40 Express, 62, 64, 87, 492

Rome's most theatrical open space got its oval shape from the Roman stadium that it's built on top of. In its centre, there's an artistic showdown between two masterpieces – the dynamic *Fountain of the Four Rivers* and the haughty Church of Sant'Agnese in Agone – by Baroque archrivals Bernini and Borromini respectively *(see p125)*.

Musei Capitolini

7 G5

Piazza del Campidoglio • 06 3996 7800 • Bus Nos. 40 Express, 62, 64, 87
» www.museicapitolini.org Open 9am–8pm Tue–Sun

A lovely alternative to the crowds at the Vatican, Michelangelo's peach-coloured palazzos form the intimate setting for some of the most important and moving works of ancient sculpture in Rome, including rare bronzes and hauntingly realistic marble portraits *(see p88)*. **Adm**

Parco Regionale dell'Appia Antica

Visitors' centre: Via Appia Antica 58–60 • 06 512 6314 • Bus Nos. 118, 218, 660
» www.parcoappiaantica.org Visitors' centre open 9:30am–5:30pm daily (Nov–Mar to 4:30); Catacombs of San Callisto open 9–noon & 2–5 Thu–Tue, closed Feb

Here, umbrella pines, crumbling ruins and grazing sheep create a rustic contrast to Rome's urban chaos. On the road itself, basalt flagstones laid in 312 BC still bear the marks of ancient cart traffic. Of the park's main catacombs, San Callisto's are the most impressive *(see p135)*.

top attractions

Fontana di Trevi `7 G1`
Piazza di Trevi • Bus Nos. 62, 95, 175, 492x

In a square barely big enough to hold it, an entire three-storey building façade is filled with this fanciful, exaggerated tableau of Neptune driving his two-seahorse chariot toward a wide pool of delightfully inviting, pale blue water. The fountain is best seen late at night, when the crowds have thinned *(see p86)*.

Spanish Steps `4 D2`
Piazza di Spagna • Ⓜ Spagna

Flanked by pink palazzos and palm trees, 138 steps of polished, curvaceous travertine cascade toward the luxury retail zone of Piazza di Spagna and Via Condotti. All day long, the sun-drenched steps are crowded with lazing Romans and the female tourists they hope to snare with the romance of the surroundings *(see p81)*.

Castel Sant'Angelo `1 D3`
Lungotevere Castello 50 • 06 681 9111 • Bus Nos. 23, 40 Express, 280
➤➤ **www.galleriaborghese.it** Open 9am–7:30pm Tue–Sun

This stout, cylindrical fortress has been a mausoleum, papal hideout and city prison. A wide spiral ramp and Renaissance staircases lead past sarcophagi and cannon balls to dramatic vistas from the ramparts. Ponte Sant'Angelo, studded with moaning and wincing angels by Bernini, connects the castle with the *centro storico (see p95)*. **Adm**

INTRODUCING ROME

You might think that religion and politics don't mix, but in Rome the edges are a little blurred and both are certainly a great excuse for a party. From the many Catholic festival days to the summer events staged by political parties, the warmer months offer myriad events held in atmospheric locations. Summer is one long, non-stop cultural feast, the highlight of which is the Estate Romana, an explosion of top-quality outdoor music, theatre, dance, cinema and literary festivals.

Settimana Santa e Pasqua
For details of events, see www.vatican.va

Easter Week draws pilgrims to Rome from all over the Catholic world. From the blessing of palms on Palm Sunday to the traditional Easter Sunday papal blessing, this is a Mass-filled week in which hundreds of thousands take part. Don't miss the Stations of the Cross ceremony held in the Colosseum on Good Friday. **Mar/Apr**

Settimana della Cultura
For details of events, see www.beniculturali.it

During this week of culture, many museums and sights are free to visit and/or stay open longer. Some collections that are normally shut to the public are opened for the occasion, and special events are organized. **Apr/May**

Primo Maggio
Piazza di San Giovanni in Laterano (Map 9 H2)
1 May, from 2pm onwards

On May Day, some 500,000 people attend a traditional free concert organized by the country's three biggest labour unions. Broadcast live on national TV, it features non-mainstream Italian bands and a few national and international stars. **May**

Festival Internazionale delle Letterature
Basilica di Massenzio, Via dei Fori Imperiali (Map 9 F1)
www.festivaldelleletterature.it

International award-winning novelists read extracts from their works under the grand arches of the old Roman Basilica of Maxentius. Paul Auster, Nadine Gordimer and Alice Sebold have all made appearances. Come early, as these free events get very crowded. **May–Jun**

Roma Incontra il Mondo
Villa Ada (Map 3 H2), www.villaada.org

A stage next to a little lake in the huge Villa Ada public park hosts musicians playing world music, as well as the odd dash of electronica, from 9pm nightly. Stands sell drinks, food from around the world, books and fair-trade products. **Jun–Aug**

spring and summer

Isola del Cinema
Isola Tiberina (Map 8 D1), www.isoladelcinema.com

An open-air cinema on the Tiber island that shows international fringe movies. Within the series, there is an Urban Islands festival for emerging directors. Bars, restaurants and market stalls are set up too. **Jun–Aug**

Estate Romana
For details of events, see www.estateromana.it

This large umbrella organization co-ordinates a wealth of cultural events ranging from ballet in the Caracalla Baths and chamber music in medieval cloisters to live open-air jazz and outdoor film screenings. **Jun–Sep**

Party Political Festivals
Various venues

People of all political affiliations attend these events, regardless of which party organizes them. Expect theatre shows and concerts, no-frills Roman food, and market stalls. The biggest is the Festa dell'Unità, organized by the Democratic Left (DS) Party in June or July. **Jun–Sep**

Cosmophonies
Ostia Antica, SW of Rome *(see p95)*, www.cosmophonies.com

Cosmophonies brings classical and contemporary performances to the ancient amphitheatre in Ostia Antica. The programme covers everything from stand-up comedy to classical Greek theatre, rock concerts and dance. **Jul**

JazzFestival a Villa Celimontana
Villa Celimontana (Map 9 G2), www.villacelimontanajazz.com

For one of Rome's best summer nights out, head to this lush and spectacularly lit villa garden. From 9pm every night, top-notch international jazz players, songwriters and dancers entertain. **Jul–Aug**

Festival EuroMediterraneo
Villa Adriana, 31 km (20 miles) NE of Rome, www.medfestival.it

The bewitching ruins of Hadrian's Villa make this festival of classical music, jazz, folk, theatre, opera, ballet and contemporary dance well worth the short trip out of town. A special bus service leaves from Via Marsala at 7pm on event days. **Jul–Aug**

INTRODUCING ROME

As the city cools down after the torrid summer months, it is time to get down to serious sightseeing, shopping, and appreciating a less-frenetic Roman lifestyle. Nevertheless, there's enough on the cultural calendar to bring extra interest to an off-season visit – from the start of the opera season to up-and-coming performance, wine-tasting and a film festival. And witnessing the Christmas celebrations in the Vatican city is certainly an experience to remember.

Enzimi
Various venues, www.enzimi.com

For two weeks, this festival showcases emerging talent in all the arts – especially theatre, music and dance – entirely free of charge. This is where Rome's most creative young things make their debuts. **Sep**

La Notte Bianca
Various venues, www.lanottebianca.it

One Saturday each year, the city's museums, libraries, bars and clubs, plus many restaurants and shops, stay open all night. Many events are also organized to coincide with La Notte Bianca ("The White Night"). **Sep/Oct**

RomaEuropa Festival
Various venues, www.romaeuropa.net

Rome's most important and coolest performing-arts festival combines new and old, cutting-edge and classic. Experimental collaborations between artforms see DJs provide the soundtracks to silent movies, and world-music bands meet techno. **Sep–Nov**

Teatro dell'Opera
7 Piazza Beniamino Gigli, (Map 5 F3), www.opera.roma.it

Autumn sees the beginning of Rome's opera season, back in the opera house after summer performances in the Caracalla Baths. The programming is varied and enterprising, and top stars regularly put in appearances. An unmissable opportunity to see the Roman cultural elite at play, and to partake in the national musical passion of a night at the opera. **Sep–Mar**

Festa Internazionale di Roma
Auditorium Parco della Musica (Mao 2 C2) and across the city
www.romacinemafest.com

A new cultural initiative is the nine-day Rome Film Festival based in Renzo Piano's impressive new Auditorium Parco della Musica. Other events take place across the city to attract the widest possible public for a feast of film. The 50 official judges are recruited from members of the public – regular cinema goers are promoted for the occasion to be allowed to make the people's choice of winners and losers. **Oct**

autumn and winter

Antiques and Craft Fairs
Via dei Coronari (Map 6 B2) and via dell'Orso (Map 6 D1)

The chic antique shops of the via dei Coronari all take part in this fair (which is repeated in May). Prices tend to be high but it's an atmospheric event with the street lit by torches. For more affordable souvenirs, check out the equally animated craft fair on the via dell'Orso. **Late Sep–Oct**

Vino Novello Wine-Tasting
Campo dei Fiori (Map 6 D4)

The Italian answer to French Beaujolais Nouveau is the local *vino novello*. These delicious light fruity wines – highly prized by the Romans – are released and enthusiastically tasted (accompanied by salami and tasty antipasti) in the city's picturesque food market. **Late Nov**

Christmas Market
Piazza Navona (Map 6 D2)

Situated in one of the most beautiful squares in Europe, this Christmas market benefits from a stunning backdrop.

Children's pleasures are very much to the fore with a merry-go-round and so many sweets and toys on display that it is difficult to play Scrooge. **Early Dec–early Jan**

Christmas Celebrations
Città del Vaticano (Map 1 B3)

The pope holds midnight Mass in St Peter's Basilica on Christmas Eve (tickets available by faxing the Prefettura della Casa Pontificia on 06 6988 5863). At noon on Christmas Day, he reads his Christmas message and blesses the crowd in St Peter's Square. **24–25 Dec**

San Silvestro and Capodanno
Piazza del Popolo (Map 4 C1) and various venues

On New Year's Eve, the city hosts a free concert and fireworks display in the Piazza del Popolo. The square in front of the Quirinale presidential palace hosts a classical-music event that is also free. On New Year's Day, a handful of men dive from Ponte Cavour into the Tiber, a dangerous but impressive tradition since 1946. **31 Dec & 1 Jan**

Central Rome is very compact, and as its narrow cobbled streets tend to complicate matters for cars and buses, the quickest – and most enjoyable – way of covering short distances is on foot. Out in the suburbs, public transport becomes much more efficient, while the quieter streets make driving or cycling a more attractive option.

Arrival

Leonardo da Vinci-Fiumicino is the larger of Rome's two airports, serving scheduled flights, while Roma Ciampino deals with charter flights and budget airlines.

Leonardo da Vinci-Fiumicino

The Leonardo Express train service is the fastest way to get into central Rome by public transport: it goes direct to Termini, where you can connect with metro lines and buses. The journey takes about 35 minutes; single tickets are under 10€. The local train service to Fara Sabina is slower but cheaper, at 5€; it stops at Trastevere, Ostiense, Tuscolana and Tiburtina. In both cases, trains leave every half hour or so between 6:30am and 11:30pm. Buy a ticket from the station ticket office or machine before boarding.

If your flight arrives too late for the trains, you can still get into Rome by night bus. Services run four times nightly between 1:15 and 5am, and cost around 5€, payable to the driver. A taxi to the city centre costs around 40€ (more at night), and takes 45 mins.

Ciampino

Rome's second airport is not as well connected. The best way to get into town on public transport is to take a bus – which runs until 11 pm – to Anagnina metro station (line A) or

Ciampino railway station for just 1€. From Anagnina it's a 30-minute ride, and from Ciampino station a 15-minute ride, to Termini. (Note that until late 2007, major engineering works mean that line A metro closes at 9pm. There is a susbstitute bus route but it is considerably slower.) Another option is to go by coach from Ciampino to Termini. **Terravision** services, run in connection with some of the budget airlines, aim to "meet" flights. However, delayed passengers may have to take the next coach. The 45-minute journey costs only 8€. Book online or buy a ticket at the desk.

If you arrive in the early hours, book a place on a coach or pay 30€ for a taxi – there are no public-transport services from Ciampino at night.

By Train

Most national and international trains come into Termini, although some early-morning or late-night services terminate at Tiburtina. Both are on the metro, but you may have to use a night bus or taxi if you arrive late. All train times and prices can be checked on the national rail website (see box).

By Coach

Eurolines coaches from across Europe and **Appian Line**'s national services terminate at Tiburtina coach station, which has good transport links.

Left Luggage

Left-luggage facilities are available at Fiumicino airport (terminal C) and at Termini (underneath platform 24).

Getting Around

Walking is the best way to get around the historical centre, but for journeys further afield, hop on to public transport, or hire a bike, car or scooter.

Public Transport

Rome's two-line metro system may seem basic, but to build more tunnels for transport would entail the destruction of ancient ruins, many of which are subterranean. The metro is best for journeys across town – otherwise, walk short distances and go by bus or tram elsewhere.

Termini is the centre of the bus, metro and train networks, and offers direct connections to almost anywhere in the city. This also applies after hours, when it becomes the terminus of most night-bus routes (marked with an N on buses and bus stops).

Tickets for all forms of public transport are available from metro stations, kiosks and newsagents displaying the **ATAC** symbol. They can't be bought on board, and you are liable for a heavy fine if caught without one. BIT tickets cost 1€ and are valid for 75 minutes, including one metro ride and as many bus and tram trips as you like within that time. They must be validated at the start of your journey in the yellow ticket machines. For unlimited travel on public transport, you can buy a daily BIG ticket (4€), or a weekly (16€) or monthly (30€) pass.

Coaches to towns and villages outside Rome are operated by Cotral. These leave from various metro and mainline stations depending on the destination. The Cotral website gives full details of routes and timetables.

Taxis

Registered taxis are yellow or white; avoid picking up unregistered taxis on the street and always check that the driver resets the meter before setting off. It's best to use taxi ranks – if you call for a cab, you will be charged for the journey the car makes to get to you.

Driving

Driving in central Rome is best avoided due to the confusing one-way systems and the inordinate amount of traffic (it's often quicker to walk), but it can be useful to hire a car for getting out of town. The authorities are tackling congestion by introducing restrictions on travel into the city centre during the week and on Saturday afternoons – you will need to apply in advance for permission to drive in the restricted zone, but your hotel should be able to help with this. Non-EU drivers must carry an international licence.

Scooters

If you want to blend in, the only way to travel is by moped. But be warned: only experienced riders should take to Rome's chaotic streets on two wheels during rush hours. There are plenty of rental places dotted around the city (try **Happy Rent**, **Scoot-a-Long** or **Scooters for Rent**). You'll need a driving licence; the price to look for is 35–50€ per day.

An Alternative

Over-18s with a valid driving licence can take to the road the eco-friendly way in one of **Free Rome's** electric buggies. These open-sided vehicles – much like golf carts – sit four and cost from 15€ for 1 hour.

Tours

The various bus, boat and walking tours of Rome are too numerous to detail here, but listings magazines and tourist offices can provide up-to-date information. A few of the more unusual tour ideas are listed below.

Horse-drawn carriages can be picked up all over the historic centre. The prices quoted tend to be expensive, but they are usually negotiable, and drivers will often adjust routes to suit your needs.

If your budget allows, experience Rome from 450m (1,500ft) above the ground on an airborne tour. **Cityfly** tours, for groups of up to nine people, take off daily from Urbe airport, last around 20 minutes and cost from 70€ per person.

If you can get a large group together, book a **Ristotram**, a vintage tram that tours Rome while you eat lunch or dinner supplied by your choice of restaurant. The tour can take up to 30 passengers, and prices start from 360€ per group excluding food.

To learn more about Rome at your own pace, rent an audio guide from **Cicerone**. In addition to two sets of earphones, you'll get a map of codes to type in for each location. The guide contains around 100 hours of information, all for just 13€ per day.

Directory

Airports
06 65 951
www.adr.it

Appian Line
06 4878 6604
www.appianline.it

ATAC
800 431 784
www.atac.roma.it

Cicerone
Cooperativa "Il Sogno",
Viale Regina Margherita 192
Map 5 H1
06 8530 1758

Cityfly
Urbe Airport, Via Salaria 825 **Map 5 F1**
06 88 333 • www.cityfly.com

Cotral
800 150 008 • www.cotralspa.it

Eurolines
055 357 110
www.eurolines.it

Free Rome
06 4201 3110
www.freerome.it

Happy Rent
Via Farini 3 **Map 5 G4**
06 481 8185

National Rail Services
892 021
www.trenitalia.com

Ristotram
Cooperativa "Il Sogno",
Viale Regina Margherita 192 **Map 5 H1**
06 8530 1758
www.mondotram.it/ristotram

Scoot-a-Long
Via Cavour 302 **Map 5 E5**
06 678 0206

Scooters for Rent
Via della Purificazione 84 **Map 5 E3**
06 488 5485

Terravision
06 7949 4572
www.terravision.it

Rome is a chaotic city – and while this adds to its charm, it can make things difficult for those with specific needs: services are often poorly documented and specialist information tends to be geared to Italian-speakers. Don't let this put you off. If you have no luck with the tourist offices, hotel staff are usually friendly, and happy to earn a tip.

Disabled Travellers

Rome's cobbled streets, crowded pavements and unpredictable traffic make things far from easy for disabled visitors. Much of metro line B is wheel-chair accessible, but much of line A is not – although bus service 590 follows the same route and is equipped to carry wheelchairs. In fact, most bus routes operate new-style vehicles with wheelchair ramps. Old buses are still in use, but not many will go by before an accessible ride arrives.

The yellow and white registered taxis are not wheelchair-accessible, but some companies have vehicles that can take wheelchairs (try **Fausta Trasporti** or **So.Me.T**).

Most of Rome's museums are at least partially accessible, although ancient sites are usually difficult to get around without help. Many of the cafés and restaurants that have step-free dining areas are let down by their inaccessible toilets. A comprehensive guide to Rome's transport, services and attractions for disabled travellers, *Roma Accessibile*, is available in several languages from **CO.IN Sociale**. This helpful organization also offers disability-related services and advice, as does **Presidio del Lazio**.

Emergencies and Health

All of Rome's hospitals have A & E departments, and are listed (as are doctors and pharmacists) in the **Pagine Gialle** (Yellow Pages). If you don't speak Italian, try the private **Rome American Hospital** (check first that your insurance covers it) or ask at your embassy, which should keep a list of English-speaking doctors.

Pharmacies operate a rota system for late opening: if the one you try is closed, it should display a sign direct-ing you to the nearest alternative.

Gay and Lesbian Travellers

Rome is not Europe's most gay-friendly city, and couples generally don't display their affection in public. There is a lively gay scene, however. A good place to start is the **Libreria Babele**, a gay and lesbian bookshop in the Ghetto and Campo dei Fiori area that stocks specialist guides and maps, and has a noticeboard where you can check out the latest events. The **Circolo Mario Mieli di Cultura Omosessuale**, **ArciGay** and **ArciLesbica** all offer listings and advice.

Listings/What's On

The weekly *Roma C'è* is published in Italian, but has a small English-language section that is worth a look. For something more substantial, try *Wanted in Rome* (a fortnightly maga-zine for the international community), which is a good source of local infor-mation and events listings, and has an online version (**www.wantedinrome.com**). The tourist office's own guide, *L'Evento*, is published every two months and can be picked up from tourist information kiosks across Rome.

Money

Where possible, change cash in banks rather than in bureaux de change, as the latter rarely offer good exchange rates, despite the enticing "no com-mission" adverts. The easiest (and often cheapest) way to get your euros is to withdraw money from an ATM. Check with your bank or credit-card supplier about commission and interest charges before you go.

Opening Hours

Restaurants and cafés have very varied opening hours. **Cafés** serving breakfast, lunch and dinner, as well as apéritifs and cocktails, usually open continu-ously from around 8am until midnight or after, while more formal **restaurants** adhere to set hours of around noon or 12:30 to 3 or 3:30pm for lunch and 7:30 or 8 to 11pm or midnight for dinner.

Shops usually open in the after-noon only on Monday, and between 9:30 or 10am and 7 or 8pm Tuesday to Saturday, with a long break for lunch. Many shops now also open for a few hours on Sundays. Food stores tend to open earlier and close later.

Although **clubs** often open at 10pm, few get busy until after midnight. Closing times range from 2 to 8am.

Most establishments are closed on the **national holidays**: 1 Jan, 6 Jan, 25 Apr, 1 May, 2 Jun, 15 Aug, 1 Nov, 8 Dec, 25 Dec, 26 Dec, Easter Monday.

Phones and Communications

Most Italians now use mobiles, but it is still easy enough to find **public phones** in airports, stations and tourist hot spots. Most of these are card-operated, and phonecards can be bought from newsagents.

If you plan to use your **mobile phone** in Rome, ask your provider about roaming costs before leaving home – or, if you plan to make a lot of local calls, buy a pre-pay Italian SIM card (make sure that your phone is not locked to your home provider or this won't work). Either way, US and Canadian visitors will need a tri-band phone to connect with an Italian network. If your phone is not compatible, it is possible to hire one. You will then need to buy credit in the same way.

You can make cheaper calls abroad with one of the many **international phonecards** (available from newsagents). These usually provide you with an access phone number and PIN, and can be used from any phone – but do watch out for connection charges and check before buying that the access number is free. Some hotels and mobile networks charge customers to call freephone numbers.

Small **Internet cafés** often provide cheap access, but computer availablity can be a problem. To get online quickly, try the centrally located **easyInternetcafé** or **The Netgate**.

The notoriously slow Italian **postal service** is improving, but it is still faster to use the Vatican system. This means buying Vatican (not Italian) stamps and posting letters within the city walls.

Security

In spite of the stories you will hear about street children and their tricks, the risk of pickpocketing is no greater in Rome than in any other city. Do, however, pay attention in crowded siutations, and keep your belongings out of the reach of passing Vespas: bag-snatching is a speciality here.

Sightseeing Permits

Some ancient sites, including Area Sacra dell'Argentina *(see p79)*, can only be visited up close with written permission. Write to Ufficio Monumenti Antichi e Scavi (Via del Portico d'Ottavio 29, 00186 Roma) stating when you'd like to go, how many people are in your party and whether the visit is for work, study or tourism.

Tipping

In Rome, service charges are usually included in the price you pay. If you eat in a restaurant where service is not included, add 10 to 15 per cent. In cafés and bars, tips are not expected, although it is normal to leave a few coins. It's also a good idea to keep some spare change for hotel staff, taxi drivers, washroom attendants and others – they usually expect 1€ or less.

Tourist Information

There is plenty of free information for visitors to pick up. The city's tourist board, **APT**, is in Via Parigi, but by far the most convenient sources of maps and leaflets are the green information kiosks (PIT) in Termini station, Via Nazionale, Piazza Pia and various other locations around the city.

Directory

APT
06 488 991
www.romaturismo.com

ArciGay
340 347 5710
www.arcigay.it

ArciLesbica
06 418 0211
www.arcilesbica/it/associazone/
presentazione.php

Circolo Mario Mieli di Cultura Omosessuale
www.mariomieli.org

CO.IN Sociale
06 2326 7504
www.coinsociale.it

easyInternetcafé
Piazza Barberini **Map 5 E3**

Fausta Trasporti
06 503 6040
www.faustatrasporti.it

Libreria Babele
Via dei Banchi Vecchi 116
Map 6 B3
06 687 6628

The Netgate
Piazza Firenze 25 **Map 7 E1**
06 687 9098
Borgo San Spirito 17 **Map 1 C3**
06 6813 4082
Stazione Termini **Map 5 G3**
06 8740 6008
www.thenetgate.it

Pagine Gialle
www.paginegialle.it

Presidio del Lazio
800 27 10 27
www.presidiolazio.it

Rome American Hospital
Via Emilio Longoni 69
Off Map; tram 5, then bus 112
06 22 551

So.Me.T
06 6618 2113
www.sometviaggi.com

restaurants

Eating out in Rome has never been so good. No longer is the menu limited to traditional Roman cuisine – the scene is increasingly rich and varied, with creative Mediterranean restaurants, Neapolitan pizza joints and a flurry of new designer eateries. But Romans are discerning diners: to make the grade here, restaurants must deliver culinary excellence, welcoming decor and first-rate service.

RESTAURANTS

The euro ended Rome's reputation for cheap dining, and family-run trattorias are being pushed into the suburbs. But the city has finally broken out of its restaurant corset: cafés, wine bars and designer eateries are on every corner and young chefs are taking risks. It's not New York, but dining at 'Gusto makes me feel more in touch with the outside world, safe in the knowledge that I can return to my local trattoria for unbeatable comfort food just like mamma makes.

Frances Kennedy

Romantic Interludes

The sheer beauty of Rome means romance is never far away. Try a touch of sensual Sicily at candlelit **Il Dito e la Luna** *(see p41)*, or enjoy an intimate dinner for two at **Taverna Angelica** *(see p47)*. For a memorable "I do" dinner, splurge at the **Hotel de Russie** *(see p39)*. The seafood delicacies on offer at **Riccioli Café** *(see p31)* always impress.

Pizza Perfect

Despite the recent popularity of the thicker-based Neapolitan pizzas, Rome's light, crunchy base still rules. **Est! Est! Est! – Da Rici** *(see p39)* serves both types, while the popular **Pizzeria Dar Poeta** *(see p47)* has created a hybrid. Bustling **Da Baffetto** *(see p30)* offers classic Roman pizza, and **Uffa Che Pizza** *(see p38)* enjoys breaking new ground.

Real Roman

The hard-core ingredient of Roman fare is still the "fifth quarter" of any beast, and offal is taken to new heights at the historic **Checchino dal 1887** *(see p43)*. More timid palates might prefer dishes such as deep-fried crispy artichokes at **Al Pompiere** *(see p33)* or creamy gnocchi and fried courgette flowers at the more humble, family-run **Da Gino** *(see p32)*.

choice eats

Eating Alfresco

With six months of summer, it pays to offer outside dining space. Want a quiet cobbled lane? Head to **Ristorarte** *(see p39)*. Prefer a bustling pavement? Try foodie hangout '**Gusto** *(see p35)*. The prize for the top piazza-restaurant combo goes to the **Trattoria San Teodoro** *(see p42)*, which serves inventive Roman fare in one of the city's quietest corners.

Gourmet Zone

Never known for pushing back culinary borders, Rome is getting bolder. Trailblazer Heinz Beck at **La Pergola** *(see p46)* has turned Italian cuisine on its head and still leads the pack. Go for a blow-out gastronomic experience with the eight-course set menu at **Agata e Romeo** *(see p39)*. **La Tana dei Golosi** *(see p41)* offers a more modest foodie adventure.

Hip Haunts

If you are eager to eat in glamorous company, funky poolside restaurant **Sette**'s *(see p38)* fusion fare is a good bet. Slick chrome interiors and top seafood draw an equally sharp and demanding clientele at **Mangiamoci** *(see p34)*, and there's always a queue at one of Rome's temples of chic, **Bloom** *(see p30)*.

Thien Kim *a taste of the Orient*

6 C5

Via Giulia 201 • 06 6830 7832
Open dinner Mon–Sat

This pioneering restaurant has been serving exquisite Vietnamese food since 1976. Ideal for a change of pace and cuisine, it has a tranquil atmosphere and courteous service. The tasty *Isola del Paradiso Verde* ("Green Island Paradise") is a seafood soup for four to share that is served over a gas burner. **Cheap**

L'Insalata Ricca *healthy option*

6 D4

Largo Chiavari 85–6 • 06 6880 3656
>> www.linsalataricca.it Open lunch & dinner daily

Plugging a gap in the market, L'Insalata Ricca serves salads in a city where meat and pasta rule. They now have eight branches around town, but this, the first, is still the best. Try the *ai gamberetti* (prawns, mushrooms, rocket and radicchio) or *la contadina* (feta cheese, olives, almonds, tomatoes and lettuce). **Cheap**

Ditirambo *gourmet destination*

6 D3

Piazza della Cancelleria 75 • 06 687 1626
>> www.ristoranteditirambo.com
Open dinner Mon, lunch & dinner Tue–Sun

Tiny Ditirambo earns top marks for gastronomic excellence, generous portions and reasonable prices. The decor is simple and rustic, with tables packed close together. It's a favourite spot of Oscar-winning actor Roberto Benigni and the lefty intellectual set, who come for dishes such as the sublime wild-mushroom ravioli with clam sauce, and the mint-flavoured gnocchi. The *piatti di mezzo* ("half plates") are generous in size and truly delicious: try the artichoke strudel or the aubergine rissoles. The menu is in Italian, English and French, and there's a good explanation (in Italian) of their superb selection of cheeses, which range from second-fermentation *gorgonzola* to alpine and cave-seasoned specialities. The wine list has a handy symbols system that describes each wine. It gets busy most evenings, so book ahead. **Moderate**

Jazz Café *live-jazz joint* `6 D2`
Via Zanardelli 12 • 06 6821 5508
Open lunch & dinner Mon–Sat

Italians may not be known for their jazz, but come to a weekend concert at the Jazz Café and you won't be disappointed. The music at this funky eatery, decked out in heavy, green velvet wall-coverings and conga-drum bar stools, is the high point. The food (pizza, pasta, steaks, burgers) is good, if unexciting. **Cheap**

Il Convivio *updated classics* `6 D1`
Vicolo dei Soldati 31 • 06 686 9432
➤➤ www.ilconviviotroiani.com Open dinner Mon–Sat

Local culinary legends the Troiani brothers revamp and play with classic dishes in their elegant but cheerful restaurant. Courgette flowers with mozzarella and anchovies are enhanced by a hot-and-sour pepper sorbet, while a caramelized, seared tuna steak is served with chestnut honey and ginger. **Expensive**

Ristorante Trattoria *modern Italian* `7 E2`
Campo Marzio Via del Pozzo delle Cornacchie 25 • 06 6830 1427
➤➤ www.ristorantetrattoria.it Open dinner Mon–Sat

The brainchild of young architects Marco and Gianluca Giammetta, Ristorante Trattoria combines modern design elements with neutral colours to create a contemporary Asian feel. Fortunately, this chic newcomer backs up its cool modern decor with exemplary food. Chef Stefano Galbiati's kitchen – visible through glass panels in the main dining room – offers eclectic *nouvelle* Italian cuisine, making use of the best regional ingredients in non-traditional ways. Menu highlights include the fried gnocchi with *culatello* (a finer version of prosciutto) and a surprisingly light lasagne with truffle-tinged meat and artichokes. Their version of the classic veal cutlet *alla Milanese* is delicious, and the fat spaghetti with chicory pesto and prawns intensely flavourful. The earnest and diplomatic sommelier won't hesitate to suggest alternative wines to match your meal. **Expensive**

➤➤ *Cheap: under 10€ for a main course; moderate: 10–15€; expensive: over 15€*

Restaurants

Da Baffetto *Roman institution* 6 C3
Via del Governo Vecchio 14 • 06 686 1617
Open dinner daily

Expect to queue at this tiny pizzeria, where Armani-clad power-brokers mix with ordinary workers. The pizzas are rigorously Roman – thin-crusted and mis-shapen – with tempting toppings. Da Baffetto draws a lively post-stadium crowd, so come after a Roma or Lazio match for the best atmosphere. **Cheap**

Casa Bleve *historic enoteca-restaurant* 6 E3
Via del Teatro Valle 48 • 06 686 5970
>> www.casableve.it Open lunch Tue–Sat, dinner Wed–Fri

The buffet served at Casa Bleve, set in a stunning palazzo with marble Apollos and wall fountains, has the feel of a sumptuous Renaissance banquet. Jovial staff help you navigate an impressive wine list and a gluttonous selection of dishes, from goat salamis to rare alpine cheeses and fish *carpaccio*. **Moderate**

Bloom *an international scene* 6 C3
Via del Teatro Pace 30 • 06 6880 2029
>> www.bloombar.it Open dinner Mon–Sat

Deep-red banquettes and low lights set a swanky tone in this 14th-century chapel-turned-ultra-hip lounge. Indulge in excellent raw fish in the upstairs sushi bar or world-class entrecôte in the ground-floor restaurant. At the latter, save room for the *feuillatine* (a chocolate dessert topped with edible gold flakes). Rome's young and fabulous hold court nightly in the wraparound Art Deco bar. **Expensive**

Ice Cream
Fruity, nutty or creamy, *gelato* is the summertime ambrosia of Rome. Although most *gelaterie* claim to make *gelato artigianale* (home-made ice cream), not all do; if a parlour's banana flavour is brown rather than lurid yellow, you've found the real thing.

Among Rome's best are **San Crispino** *(see p178)*, which only serves *gelato* in tubs, because the proprietors believe that cones contaminate the flavour. Big, old and full of character, **Il Palazzo del Freddo di Giovanni Fassi** *(see p178)* makes sublime ice cream; try the *riso gelato* (made from rice) or the white-chocolate flavour. Popular with MPs from the nearby parliament, **Giolitti** *(see p178)* is a *gelato* institution and an obligatory stop on any stroll through the centre of Rome.

Obikà *trendy mozarella bar* `7 E1`
Via dei Prefetti 26A • 06 683 2630
» www.obika.it Open breakfast, lunch & dinner daily

Inspired by sushi-lovers' reverence for raw ingredients, Obikà's focus is not fish but mozarella, which is treated with the utmost respect by its white-gloved waiters. Try the simple *fior di latte* or creamy *burrata* served with tomatoes and salami. A great-value 10€ set lunch draws nearby workers. **Moderate**

Riccioli Café *champagne and oyster bar* `7 E1`
Piazza delle Coppelle 10a • 06 6821 0313
» www.larosetta.com Open lunch & dinner Mon–Sat

This oyster bar on a charming cobblestoned piazza is the trendy spawn of La Rosetta, Rome's most venerable seafood restaurant. The oysters – direct from Brittany – are divine, the sushi is awesomely fresh and the seafood kebabs are tender. Hot young things come for oyster Martinis at happy hour. **Expensive**

Il Bicchiere di Mastai *simple but effective* `6 B2`
Via dei Banchi Nuovi 52 • 06 6819 2228
» www.laltromastai.com Open lunch & dinner daily

A welcoming wine bar that offers creative soups, pastas and salads is a real find in Rome. The decor is inviting, with marble and wrought-iron tables lit by candles in the evening. The lunch menu is excellent value and at least 20 of the 300 wines on offer are available by the glass. **Expensive**

La Caffettiera *Neapolitan sweet treats* `7 F2`
Piazza della Pietra 65 • 06 679 8147
Open breakfast, lunch & early dinner daily

The Neapolitan food here surpasses most café fare. Don't miss the *rustici* (savoury pastries) or the *timballo* (baked pasta), and leave room for a delicious *babà al rhum* or the *sfogliatelle* (a ricotta-filled pastry best with coffee). This is a popular spot for a quick lunch. **Cheap**

Restaurants

Sora Lella *prime island spot* `8 D1`
Via di Ponte Quattro Capi 16, Isola Tiberina • 06 686 1601
» www.soralella.com Open lunch & dinner Mon–Sat

It's not just the warm hospitality and hearty Roman fare that makes Sora Lella so special – it's also the location on romantic Tiber Island. Lella, the founder, has passed away, but her son keeps her culinary reputation alive with knockout dishes like *paccheri* (fat pasta tubes) stuffed with fish and aubergines. **Expensive**

Osteria dell'Ingegno *a slice of the Med* `7 F2`
Piazza di Pietra 45 • 06 678 0662
Open lunch & dinner Mon–Sat

A well-heeled clientele frequents this informal, stylish *osteria*, which serves well-executed Mediterranean cuisine. The changing menu may include warm buffalo ricotta with grilled vegetables, tartare of salmon and *spigola* (sea bass), or *tortelli* with chestnuts and goat's cheese in red wine. **Expensive**

Da Gino *Roman home cooking* `7 E1`
Vicolo Rosini 4 • 06 687 3434
Open lunch & dinner Mon–Sat

White-jacketed waiters and crazy floral frescoes set the scene for Mamma's no-frills Roman cooking. Gnocchi, tripe, oxtail and cod make regular weekly appearances on the specials menu. The handmade *tonnarelli* (a long, square-cut pasta) and the crème caramel is always excellent. **Cheap**

Enoteca Corsi *good food, great wine* `7 F3`
Via del Gesù 87 • 06 679 0821
Open lunch Mon–Sat

This historic wine shop stops selling bottles at lunchtime just as the kitchen swings into operation. Paper tablecloths, blackboard menus and low-key service mark it out as one of the last genuine Roman taverns. Home-made pastas are hearty, mains tasty, especially the *saltimbocca alla romana* (pan-fried veal). **Cheap**

Le Bain *style central* `7 F4`
Via delle Botteghe Oscure 32 • 06 686 5673
»» **www.lebain.it** Open lunch & dinner Mon–Sat

A former fencing gym, Le Bain is one of Rome's hippest and most vibrant restaurant-lounges. Its decor fuses comfort and glamour, with warm lighting and art-clad walls. The food and drink are equally luxurious; champagne flows and dishes like entrecôte with espresso sauce are as velvety as the banquettes. **Expensive**

Piperno *Roman-Jewish cooking* `7 E5`
Via Monte dei Cenci 9 • 06 6880 6629
»» **www.ristorantepiperno.it** Open lunch & dinner Tue–Sat

Piperno has been serving brilliant food for decades. Highlights include *carciofi alla giudea* (deep-fried artichokes) and *pasta e ceci* (with chickpeas). Finish off with the *palle del nonno* (literally "grandpa's balls"), made from ricotta cheese. There are tables outside in summer. **Expensive**

Sora Margherita *basic but unbeatable* `7 E5`
Piazza delle Cinque Scole 30 • 06 687 4216
Open summer: lunch Mon–Fri, dinner Fri;
winter: lunch Tue–Sun, dinner Fri & Sat

Don't dismiss this place on appearance, as its hearty portions of home-made classics, including some Jewish dishes, are hard to beat. There's no sign outside and the daily-changing menu is scribbled on a piece of paper: welcome to a true Roman canteen. **Cheap**

Al Pompiere *local classics* `7 E5`
Palazzo Cenci Via Santa Maria dei Calderari 38 • 06 686 8377
Open lunch & dinner Mon–Sat (closed late Jul–Sep)

Under frescoed ceilings in an old palazzo, relaxed Pompiere offers a mainly Roman-Jewish menu, with a handful of other Italian dishes. The gnocchi and the *straccetti* (beef strips with rocket) are both excellent, as are the desserts. Try the *torta della nonna*, with creamy ricotta and pine nuts. **Moderate**

Restaurants

Il Margutta Ristorarte *bold vegetarian* 4 C2

Via Margutta 118 • 06 3265 0577
>> www.ilmargutta.it
Open lunch & dinner daily (closed 10 days in Aug)

Vibrant colours, leather sofas and cutting-edge art exhibitions make this vegetarian restaurant a happening rendezvous even for carnivores. The pioneering owners are stamping out the myth that vegetarian cuisine is dull with an impressive *degustazione* (tasting) menu (36€). Dishes combine the best (mainly organic) Mediterranean ingredients: filo-pastry baskets are filled with spinach and mushrooms on a bed of celery and pumpkin, and a Parmesan crust is heaped with steamed baby vegetables tossed in olive oil. All the bread, pasta and sweets are made in-house and the cheeseboard focuses on a different Italian region each day. There's an excellent wine list too, plus a range of organic ciders and beers. The 15€ weekday set lunch is excellent value; the busy Sunday-brunch buffet has a good selection for 25€. **Moderate**

Mangiamoci *seafood galore* 4 D2

Salita di San Sebastianello • 06 678 0546
Open lunch Tue–Sun

Trendy Mangiamoci has an all-encompassing menu, from basic salads to elaborate seafood dishes – live lobsters can be picked from the crustacea tank. The interior is high-tech, colourful and brightly lit, with a popular bar area featuring soft blue leather ottomans and poufs. **Moderate**

Pizza

Plain unadorned pizza base with just a touch of oil and salt – *pizza bianca* – is the archetypal Roman fast food, guaranteed to fill that mid-morning or late-afternoon carbohydrate gap. There are plenty of *pizza al taglio* (pizza by the slice) outlets around the capital and most bakeries sell pizza, too. Split open and stuffed with cheese, vegetables or ham, *pizza bianca* can also make a wholesome lunch. Some of the best fillings and toppings are seasonal, though *pizza con le patate* (topped with matchstick-sliced potatoes) is a year-round favourite. Most places serve good pizza, but the top spots are **Fantasia del Pane** (see p172), which is always crowded at lunchtime, and bakeries **Forno di Campo dei Fiori** (see p57) and **Panella, L'Arte del Pane** (see p69).

'Gusto *multiple dining options* `4 C2`

Piazza Augusto Imperatore 9 • 06 322 6273

>> www.gusto.it Open lunch & dinner daily

Ten years after it first leapt enthusiastically on to the Roman restaurant scene, this eating emporium is still hip, and hugely popular. The decor is composed of bare beams and industrial fittings, and the immense shaded area outside means there is ample alfresco dining space with complementary blankets when it's chilly. Service can be a little off-hand at times, but the place has a pleasing buzz and the food is excellent.

'Gusto tries to cover a lot of culinary ground: there is a ground-floor pizzeria, an upstairs restaurant offering creative Mediterranean-Italian fare, a wonderful wine shop, a wine bar offering tasty snacks throughout the day and one of the best-stocked kitchenware and foodie bookshops around *(see p64)*. The wine bar has live music late in the evening, with jazz, soul and occasional improvised jam sessions.

The latest addition to the 'Gusto empire is the Osteria della Frezza (entrance on Via della Frezza 16), where, as well as full meals, you can have *cicchetti* (mini tapas-style portions) of any of the dishes on the main menu. You can enjoy five *cicchetti* and a glass of wine for under 10€.

The *formaggeria* works both as a cheese shop and a spot to sit down with a glass of wine and a slice; if you ask nicely, they'll show you the cheese-ageing rooms downstairs, which can also be hired for private functions. **Expensive**

Pizza Rè *Naples-style pizza*

Via di Ripetta 14 • 06 321 1468
Open lunch & dinner daily

This Neapolitan joint, and its several branches, has won over many locals who were convinced their Roman-style super-thin pizzas were superior. Always busy, Rè offers classic toppings on thicker bases, plus some other Neapolitan specialities, such as buffalo mozzarella and *friarielli* (bitter broccoli). **Cheap**

Le Bistrot d'Hubert *French classics* 5 F1

Via Sardegna 135 • 06 4201 3161
Open lunch & dinner Mon–Fri, dinner Sat

The eponymous Hubert has recreated a typical Paris bistro just off Via Veneto, in the heart of Rome. French classics, such as vichyssoise and the more humble *croque monsieur*, are prepared with care and a little less butter than the French originals, so as not to scare off calorie-conscious Italians. There is also a range of French regional dishes that is changed regularly. Hubert hand-picks the cheeses, cold cuts and wines – all available by the glass – from small producers on his frequent buying trips to France. The atmosphere and service are fairly formal in the evening, when loving couples indulge in classics such as onion soup, fillet steak with pepper sauce and apple tart. Lunch is slightly more relaxed, as businessmen come to talk shop and ladies do lunch over omelettes and salads. *Chanson* and other French music adds to the romantic mood. **Moderate**

Enoteche with Good Food

The quality of Italian wines has improved in recent years, so Italians have become more appreciative of their domestic output. This is evidenced by the explosion of *enoteche* in Rome. Some are excellent wine shops, such as **Buccone** *(see p178)*, where you can taste various wines and nibble on snacks. A few, such as **Enoteca Ferrara** *(see p71)* and **Enoteca**

Capranica are full-blown restaurants with mind-bogglingly huge wine lists. Most are wine bars offering cheeses, salamis and light meals at reasonable prices. **Trimani Enoteca** *(see p68)* and two other historic *enoteche* – **Cavour 313** *(see p178)* and **Cul de Sac** *(see p178)* – have kept their reputations and clientele amid the newcomers. **Costantini** *(see p178)* has top-notch cuisine and a massive cellar.

Da Settimio all'Arancio *home-made* `4 C3`
Via dell' Arancio 50 • 06 687 6119
Open lunch & dinner daily

The owners of this trattoria make their own bread, pasta and *pizza bianca (see p34)*. The food is traditional Italian, with Roman specialities and juicy steaks cooked on heated stone plates. The central location, efficient service and affordability make it popular with journalists from nearby newspaper offices. **Moderate**

Le Pain Quotidien *delicious baked goods* `4 C3`
Via Tomacelli 24–5 • 06 6880 7727
»» www.lepainquotidien.com
Open breakfast & lunch daily

At this bakery-restaurant, diners eat sandwiches, soups, salads and light meals around large communal wooden tables. In good weather, tables are put outside on the pretty terrace. The American-style Sunday brunch is very popular. **Cheap**

Al Presidente *top-notch seafood* `7 H1`
Via in Arcione 95 • 06 679 7342
»» www.alpresidente.it Open lunch & dinner Tue–Sun

Prior to the death of their *papà*, the Allegrini family ran a typical tourist restaurant. They have now relaunched it as a first-class Italian seafood and fish eatery, to much acclaim. The quality of the dishes, the attention to detail and the pleasant service are worth paying for. There's a 18€ buffet. **Expensive**

Sora Lucia *Trevi tradition* `7 H1`
Via della Panetteria 41a • 06 679 4078
Open lunch & dinner daily

Diners expecting traditional red-checked tablecloths and classic Roman recipes will not be disappointed here. Dishes include *bucatini all'amatriciana* (with tomato and bacon sauce) and *saltimbocca* (veal escalopes cooked in wine with Parma ham and sage leaves). The Trevi fountain is close by. **Moderate**

Café Renault *modish dining* `5 E4`
Via Nazionale 183b • 06 4782 4452
Open lunch Mon–Sat, dinner Tue–Sun (Jul–Aug: closed Sun)

This spacious café, owned by the French car company, serves modern Italian food. At lunchtime, the self-serve area is is full of office workers; in the evenings, it gets buzzier as the upstairs dining room fills with locals sampling the likes of *pappardelle* with wild boar sauce. The downstairs bar has occasional jazz. **Moderate**

Restaurants

Sette *upscale chic* `5 H4`
Radisson SAS ES.Hotel Via Filippo Turati 171 • 06 444 841
>> www.rome.radissonsas.com
Open lunch & dinner daily (booking essential)

A glamorous crowd is lured by Sette's sleek poolside dining room. The menu favours bold combinations such as warm rabbit *carpaccio* with fried fish in a balsamic-vinegar caramel. The wine list features up-and-coming and organic labels. **Expensive**

Uffa Che Pizza *pizza parlour*
Via dei Taurini 39 • 06 445 3306 • Tram Nos. 3 & 19 to Reti
Open lunch Mon–Fri, dinner Mon–Sat

Noisy but fun, this pizzeria is a terrific find. Order the *coccodrillo*, a long skinny calzone, or the *pizza palla*, which is puffed up with air to make a ball. Interesting – sometimes adventurous – toppings are served up alongside classics; brie and radicchio, and gorgonzola and rocket are both winners. **Cheap**

Hostaria degli Artisti *Neapolitan gem* `10 B1`
Via Germano Sommeiller 6 • 06 701 8148
Open lunch & dinner Mon–Sat; winter: also open lunch Sun

The friendly Artisti is home to the rich cuisine of Naples. Highlights on the daily changing menu include pasta *alla genovese* with an onion sauce, *polpette* (meatballs) and *impepata di cozze* (sautéed black mussels). Leave room for the *pastiera Napoletana* (cake filled with ricotta and candied fruit). **Moderate**

Colline Emiliane *outstanding trattoria* `5 E3`
Via degli Avignonesi 22 • 06 481 7538
Open lunch Tue–Sun, dinner Tue–Sat

A little piece of the Emilia-Romagna region has been transported to this intimate and welcoming trattoria. A meat tortellini in *brodo* (broth) makes the perfect starter. Serious carnivores should then choose *bollito* (simmered meats served with sauce and mustards) washed down with a regional wine. **Moderate**

Est! Est!! Est!!! – Da Ricci *pizza pizzaz*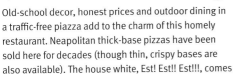

Via Genova 32 • 06 488 1107
Open dinner Tue–Sun

Old-school decor, honest prices and outdoor dining in a traffic-free piazza add to the charm of this homely restaurant. Neapolitan thick-base pizzas have been sold here for decades (though thin, crispy bases are also available). The house white, Est! Est!! Est!!!, comes in both *secco* (dry) and *amabile* (medium). **Cheap**

Agata e Romeo *for gourmets*   5 G4

Via Carlo Alberto 45 • 06 446 6115
>> www.agataeromeo.it Open lunch & dinner Mon–Fri

Romeo (maître d') and Agata (chef) may no longer be the unrivalled king and queen of Roman haute cuisine, but their restaurant is still a magnet for serious food-lovers with serious cash. Opt for the traditional set menu, or make a night of it with the eight-course gastronomic menu, which is paired with four wines. **Expensive**

Trattoria Monti *Roman favourite*   5 G5

Via San Vito 13 • 06 446 6573
Open lunch Tue–Sun, dinner Tue–Sat

A small neighbourhood trattoria, Monti offers Roman cuisine with a nod to the Marche region. Specialities include the *tortello al rosso d'uovo* (a giant tortellini stuffed with ricotta, spinach and egg yolk) and *minestra al sacco* (vegetable broth). It's a popular after-show haunt with members of the city opera. **Moderate**

Sunday Brunch

With many young Romans tiring of marathon Sunday lunches with the family, restaurant brunches are now *de rigueur*. Italian-style brunch usually means freshly squeezed orange juice, *torte rustiche* (savoury tarts), salads, pizza and light pasta dishes; it's more of a lunch than a breakfast and not usually served before 11:30am. *'Gusto (see p35)* has Italian-American brunch options and **Ristorarte** *(see p34)* has a popular 25€ vegetarian buffet brunch. For a special occasion, the garden restaurant at the **Hotel de Russie** *(see p142)* is unbeatably romantic. If you want the whole British bacon-and-eggs thing, try one of the pubs that dot the city, such as **Trinity College** *(see p170)* ; for American pancakes, head to **Ristorante Bramante** *(see p178)*.

Restaurants

Africa *authentic African*

5 G2

Via Gaeta 26 • 06 494 1077
Open lunch & dinner Tue–Sun

This genuine, laid-back and friendly eatery offers classic dishes from Italy's former colonies, Eritrea and Ethiopia. There's no cutlery; instead, a large spongy pancake – called an *ingera* – is used to scoop up the food, which includes a delicious, but spicy, *zighinì* (mutton stew). It's cash only here. **Cheap**

Arancia Blu *creative vegetarian*

Via dei Latini 55–65 • 06 445 4105 • Bus Nos. 71, 204, 492
Open lunch Sun, dinner daily

The mission of this soft-lit, dark wood-panelled restaurant is to lift the stigma attached to vegetarian dining. Hearty and satisfying dishes include lasagne with wild asparagus and Castelmagno cheese, and nut ravioli with a Parmesan and rosemary sauce. The four-course fixed-price menu is a bargain at 28€. **Moderate**

F.I.S.H. *fantastic fish*

5 E5

Via dei Serpenti 16 • 06 4782 4962
» www.f-i-s-h.it Open lunch & dinner Tue–Sun

The Fine International Seafood House certainly lives up to its name, serving sumptuous sea produce from as far away as the South Pacific. Top-notch sushi, seafood platters and Asian dishes such as *nasi goreng* and *pad thai*, are made only from the freshest – and finest – seafood. The signature dish *vulcano di riso nero* ("black-rice volcano") uses a three-rice mix to lightly cook the enclosed seafood; the resulting flavours are delicate beyond belief.

   A sleek, design-conscious space – all geometric shapes and perspex – is split into three: a grill room, a sushi bar and an *acqua* bar (for an unrivalled selection of mineral waters). The menu also has three sections, with Mediterranean, Oriental and Oceanic (commonly known as Pacific Rim) offerings. An open kitchen allows diners to watch the chefs work their magic. Take-out sushi is also available. **Expensive**

Il Dito e la Luna *Sicilian romance*

Via dei Sabelli 51 • 06 494 0726 • Bus Nos. 71, 204, 492
Open dinner Mon–Sat

A little corner of Sicily in San Lorenzo, this discreet restaurant oozes romance. Favourite dishes include marinated orange and onion salad, and pasta *con le sarde* (with sardines, breadcrumbs, pine nuts and orange peel). The *caponata*, a sweet-and-sour aubergine salad, paired with Sicilian wine, is sublime. **Moderate**

Domenico dal 1968 *down-to-earth local* `10 A4`

Via Satrico 23 • 06 7049 4602
Open lunch Tue–Sat, dinner Mon–Sat

The portions at this small, simple neighbourhood trattoria are generous and well priced. Roman classics and more adventurous creations feature on the short menu. Pasta *all'amatriciana* – a spicy tomato sauce with *guanciale* (pork cheek) – and its tomato-less equivalent, *alla gricia*, are both exceptional. **Moderate**

La Tana dei Golosi *the finer things in life* `9 H1`

Via di San Giovanni in Laterano 220 • 06 7720 3202
» www.latanadeigolosi.it Open dinner Mon–Sat

La Tana was lovingly created by a bunch of foodie friends with a passion for Italy's rich culinary traditions. The menu changes twice a month to focus on a different regional cuisine and a different period in history. Friends and avid followers come to feast on concoctions such as quail roasted in laurel or Habsburg goulash – both from Lombardy – or Papal States dishes like *tagliolini* with nettle and prawns, and cod with sweet peppers. Much of the produce is organic, and all the ingredients are of an exceptionally high quality. For instance, the owners only cook with the olive oil produced from their own olive grove. A simple, almost spartan, interior allows the food to speak for itself. An extensive wine list representing all the key Italian wine-growing regions (and offering excellent value for money) also marks this out as a serious eatery. **Moderate**

Restaurants

Trattoria San Teodoro *food innovation* 9 E1
Via dei Fienili 49–51 • 06 678 0933
Open lunch & dinner Mon–Sat

In a tranquil, cobbled square surrounded by medieval palazzos, this sophisticated dining spot offers Roman cuisine with a twist, and with a strong seafood slant. The interior successfully combines the old with the new: original vaulted brick ceilings are complemented by a chic black marble floor and artworks by leading contemporary Roman painters. In the warmer months, alfresco dining in Rome's prettiest (traffic-free) piazza is the draw. The charming setting and attentive, but not-too-formal, service make this ideal for either a romantic dinner or a business lunch.

Among the starters, the raw-fish dishes shine, particularly the sea-bass *carpaccio* and the tuna tartare. Fried buffalo ricotta cheese with chicory flowers is also worthy of attention. The *primi piatti* vary from a traditional *cacio e pepe* (*pecorino* sheep's cheese and black pepper) to spaghetti with scampi, a shaving of *pecorino* and courgette blossoms. Freshen your palate between courses with the inimitable wild-fennel sorbet. The emphasis on fish continues in the main courses, where grilled red mullet with fish roe is a favourite. Carnivorous offerings include finely sliced, lightly grilled beef served with artichoke chips.

The pastry chef has a passion for chocolate, so there's plenty on the dessert menu, as well as an interesting *gelato* interpretation of the Sicilian *cassata* cake and a ricotta ice cream in a tasty tart, with dried fruit and whipped cream. An ambitious drinks list rounds things off, with established wines from across Italy as well as from up-and-coming producers, plus a good selection of whiskies and liqueurs. **Expensive**

Checchino dal 1887 *carnivorous feasting* `8 C4`
Via di Monte Testaccio 30 • 06 574 3816
>> www.checchino-dal-1887.com Open lunch & dinner Tue–Sat

This classy restaurant is as authentically Roman as you'll get. Located opposite the city's former slaughterhouse, Checchino specializes in the *quinto quarto* ("fifth quarter") – that is, the bits that are left over once the four main quarters of a carcass have been used. Traditional dishes, such as sweetbreads with tripe and a historic recipe for stewed donkey meat with cloves, are served here, to much local acclaim. These and other Roman classics, like pasta *e fagioli* (with beans), have, however, been modified for milder modern tastes.

There's a 600-strong selection of wines, with many non-Italian names, all of which are stored in the impressive cellar. Built into the Monte dei Cocci, an artificial hill composed of ancient Roman amphora shards, the cellars can be visited by diners wishing to peruse the many bottles on offer. **Expensive**

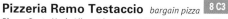

Pizzeria Remo Testaccio *bargain pizza* `8 C3`
Piazza Santa Maria Liberatrice 44 • 06 574 6270
Open dinner Mon–Sat

It's boisterous, it's popular and you sure get a lot of pizza for your euro. As well as the larger-than-life pizzas, there's Roman fast food such as *supplì* (fried rice balls) and *fiori di zucca* (fried courgette flowers with mozzarella and anchovies). Come early or late to avoid queues, and expect some table-sharing. **Cheap**

Tutti Frutti *creative casual cuisine* `8 D4`
Via Luca della Robbia 3A • 06 5757 902
Open dinner Tue–Sun

Staff at this casual, arty restaurant are genuinely welcoming and enthusiastic about its innovative Italian cuisine. The daily-changing menu is small but select with some stars such as *carpaccio* of sea bass with raw artichokes and "cold" roast pork with tangy apricot chutney. **Cheap**

Da Bucatino *hearty home cooking* `8 D3`
Via Luca della Robbia 84–6 • 06 5746 886
Open lunch & dinner Tue–Sun

This tiny trattoria with its kitsch decor, film-star photos and genuine Roman home cooking is a real treasure, so book ahead or risk disappointment. Classics such as *tonarelli cacio e pepe* (pasta with cheese and pepper) and *coda alla vaccinara* (oxtail) are always delicious. Service is friendly but not fussy. **Cheap**

>> Alimentari *are delicatessens*, forni *are bakeries for bread and* pasticceria *are cake shops*

Restaurants

Il Cortile *a real find* `8 A3`
Via Alberto Mario 25 • 06 580 3433
Open lunch Tue–Sun, dinner Tue–Sat

The buffet of 20 fresh vegetable appetizers is a major draw at this local gem, which attracts a loyal following. Alfresco dining, affable owners, traditional Italian and Roman mains and to-die-for desserts add to the appeal. *Tiramisù* comes in three styles – classic, orange liqueur, or *vin santo* and fresh berries. **Moderate**

The Kitchen *gourmet treat* `8 D4`
Via dei Conciatori 3 • 06 574 1505
Open lunch Mon–Fri, dinner Mon–Sat

Run by fine-food pioneers Maria and Raffaella, this casual eatery in Ostiense has wooden floors, minimalist decor and an open kitchen. The young chef, who trained in some of the city's top spots, skilfully plays with seasonal produce in dishes such as *carpaccio* of octopus with fennel and anchovies. **Moderate**

Ristorante Asinocotto *welcoming bistro* `8 D1`
Via dei Vascellari 48 • 06 589 8985
» www.asinocotto.com Open dinner Tue–Sun

Rome's only self-proclaimed gay-friendly restaurant resembles an intimate French brasserie. Emerging chef and owner Giuliano Brenna shows creative flair: try tagliatelle with seafood, black olives and marjoram to start, followed by swordfish with capers and citrus fruits. Daily specials are made with market-fresh ingredients and there's a carefully chosen 300-strong wine list. **Expensive**

Da Vittorio *quintessential Roman pizza* `8 C1`
Via di San Cosimato 14a • 06 580 0353
Open dinner Tue–Sun

Da Vittorio is a salt-of-the-earth Roman pizzeria: imagine checked tablecloths, straw-covered wine casks and celebrity photos on the walls. The heart-shaped pizza Maradona (dedicated to the Argentinian footballer) and pizza Mondiale (World Football Championship) show the owners' love of the game. **Cheap**

Città del Gusto *gastronomic mecca*

Via Enrico Fermi 161 • 06 551 121 • Bus No. 170
>> www.gamberorosso.it
L'Osteria del Gambero Rosso: open lunch Mon, lunch & dinner
Tue–Fri, dinner Sat Teatro del Vino: open dinner Tue–Sat

This huge grain warehouse was transformed into the
"City of Taste" by Italy's most prominent food-and-
wine organization, Gambero Rosso, which publishes
food and wine books and gives quality ratings to
restaurants, wine bars and food shops across Italy.

Inside the sleek steel-and-chrome building, diners
have two choices. The cosy Teatro del Vino wine bar is
on the top floor, where there's a separate wine-
tasting room for sampling some of the vast stock of
quality domestic wines. The small, select menu of
creative Italian dishes changes daily, and there are
delicious snack options available, too. A huge terrace
here affords an amazing view of industrial Rome. The
alternative option is L'Osteria del Gambero Rosso, on
the second floor, where the focus is on a small menu
of tasty dishes. Salads, pastas and a few mains – all
at competitive prices – are paired with good wines at
just 3€ a glass. In the evenings, you can watch the
pizzaiolo (pizza-maker) at work.

What really makes this place buzz, however, are the
added extras: a food-related satellite TV channel
transmits from here; there are cooking and wine-
tasting courses (some in English); Italy's most
dynamic chefs can be seen at work in the *teatro della
cucina* (theatre of cooking), where some of their
dishes can be sampled. And there's even a book and
cookware emporium next door where you can buy
state-of-the-art cooking accessories to help you
recreate the dishes back home. **Moderate**

La Pergola *pure indulgence*

Hotel Cavalieri Hilton, Via Cadlolo 101 • 06 3509 2055
Ⓜ Ottaviano, or hotel's own shuttle bus to/from city centre
➤➤ www.cavalieri-hilton.it Open dinner Tue–Sat

Heinz Beck is the German culinary genius who has elevated the restaurant in the ugly hilltop Hilton to Rome's gastronomic peak. Obsessive, imaginative and uncompromising, only one in ten of the dishes that Beck tries out makes it on to the menu. This has helped him win over even the most exacting food critics. The seven-course *menù degustazione* (145€) allows you to fully appreciate Heinz's mastery of Mediterranean haute cuisine. Culinary creations include green tortellini with clams and baby calamari, and black truffle risotto with apple and smoked foie gras. His signature dish is courgette flowers fried in a thin, almost transparent, saffron batter, served with courgette purée and a quail egg. Beck, who generally strives to keep his cooking super-light, indulges with desserts, offering a "seven sins" platter with tiny portions of seven sweets. There's a splendid cheese trolley boasting 20 of Italy's rarest regional specialities and the award-winning sommelier is on hand to recommend wines (guests can also visit the impressive wine cellar).

Topping off the experience, the elegant restaurant offers a dining terrace with a commanding view of the city below. But all of this comes at a price – it's unlikely you'll get out of the door without spending at least 120€ a head. Book online at least one month in advance, and dress formally (jacket and tie). **Expensive**

Taverna Angelica *a taste of the Med* `1 C3`
Via Piazza Amerigo Capponi 6 • 06 687 4514
>> www.tavernaangelica.it Open lunch Sun, dinner daily

It's unusual to find a quality eatery near the Vatican, so this small, contemporary and atmospheric spot is a rare find. Food is Mediterranean and top marks go to the *cavatelli* pasta with lamb, almond and aubergine sauce, and the turbot in *cartoccio* (cooked in foil in its own juices). The ice creams are simply sublime. **Moderate**

Da Guido *seasonal menu* `8 B1`
Via della Scala 31a • 06 580 0733
Open lunch & dinner Mon–Wed, Fri–Sun

The owner's Tuscan origins show through in this restaurant's no-nonsense approach and dedication to seasonal produce. The fettucine *ai carciofi* (with artichokes) is exceptional, as is the Danish beef, in the form of tartare, steak or fillet. Outside tables are a little noisy, but perfect for people-watching. **Moderate**

Pizzeria Dar Poeta *poetic pizza* `8 B1`
Vicolo del Bologna 45 • 06 588 0516
>> www.darpoeta.it Open dinner daily

Dedicated to local poet Belli, this pizzeria is wildly popular. The pizza base here is a hybrid of the Roman and Neapolitan schools – crispy but slightly thicker around the edges. The owners claim that the special flour mix makes it more digestible too. Sweet *calzoni* include the sinful chocolate and ricotta dessert. **Cheap**

Zen *top-notch Japanese* `1 C2`
Via degli Scipioni 243 • 06 321 3420
>> www.zenworld.it Open lunch Tue–Fri & Sun, dinner Tue–Sun

A loyal clientele of Japanese expats is evidence that there's more to sleek, minimalist Zen than Rome's first *kaiten-sushi* (conveyor belt) restaurant. Sushi and sashimi in traditional wooden boats, exquisite flash-grilled tuna and salmon, and masterful *miso* soup are just a few of the delectable offerings. **Moderate**

>> *For an index of restaurants by types of cuisine,* see pp178–9

shopping

Style is everything here, and Romans spend serious time and money to achieve the elegant sophistication of *bella figura*. While the fashion scene in Rome is not quite on the same scale as Milan, there are plenty of options to keep shoppers happy. From leather goods handmade in artisan work-shops to designer three-piece suits, expect the highest quality – whatever you buy.

SHOPPING

Like an archaeologist, you will have to dig a little to discover Rome's shopping treasures. As the fashion retail scene is dominated by independent shops devoted to one label, you might have to spend more time shopping around than in other cities. For big-name Italian designers and some serious window shopping you won't need to venture far from the Spanish Steps, but you might miss out on some of the enticing diversity that Rome has to offer.

Sally Washington

Retail Hot Spot – Via del Govorno Vecchio

This narrow cobblestoned street in Navona contains some of Rome's best boutiques. Local designer Patrizia Pieroni sells her sought-after, sleek and elegant creations at **Arsenale** *(see p52)*. For well-chosen international and Italian designer fashion check out **L'una e l'altra** (No. 75) and both stores of **Josephine de Huertas** (No. 59 and No. 68).

One-Stop Style

If your time is limited, head to one of the city's few shops that stock the work of several designers. **TAD** *(see p62)* is Rome's first concept store (stocking fashion, shoes and homewares), while the range of shoes and accessories at **NuYorica** *(see p54)*, and fashion labels at **Campo de' Fiori 52** *(see p54)* make them similarly popular with fashionistas.

Must-Have Accessories

Italians pride themselves on being well shod (just notice how they check out your footwear). If your budget can't stretch to **Bottega Veneta** *(see p53)* or **Sergio Rossi** *(see p61)*, then try **Fausto Santini** *(see p62)* for truly wonderful leatherwear. Also, the hip yet affordable bags, wallets and luggage at **Mandarina Duck** *(see p61)* seem to last forever.

choice shops

Eat, Drink, Be Merry

Rome's *alimentari* (groceries) offer a feast for the eyes as well as the stomach. Head to **Volpetti** *(see p70)* for one of the finest selections in town (you can try before you buy), or to **Trimani Enoteca** *(see p68)*, which sells an extensive selection of wine; both stores will ship your purchases. Buzzy **Campo dei Fiori** *(see p67)* is the pick of the outdoor markets.

Italian Interiors

Italian style extends to the home. From funky and functional Alessi pieces to colourful Amalfi crockery, **Modigliani** *(see p61)* is a good bet. At **'Gusto** *(see p64)* you'll find kitchen gadgets and pasta paraphernalia. But for something truly special with a bit of history to boot, the vintage housewares at **Retrò** *(see p60)* are worth seeking out.

Modish Menswear

Emulate stylish Roman men and spruce up your wardrobe. For a quintessential Italian look you can't better **Ermenegildo Zegna** *(see p61)*, but the designs at **SBU** *(see p53)* and cool labels at **empresa** *(see p54)* are much more edgy. **Cravatterie Nationale** *(see p63)* has ties for everyone with its range of daring and more traditional designs.

Shopping

Ai Monasteri *holy provisions* 6 D2
Corso del Rinascimento 72 • 06 6880 2783
Open 9am–7:30pm Mon–Sat

Just a stone's throw from Piazza Navona, this outlet offers handmade comforts direct from a Cistercian monastery. Shelves are laden with soaps and lotions, and there are mouth-watering displays of jams, chocolate and *torrone*. The liqueurs, prepared according to an ancient recipe, make fine souvenirs.

Le Tartarughe *exclusive ladieswear* 7 F3
Main shop: Via Piè di Marmo 17 • 06 679 2240
Accessories: Via Piè di Marmo 33 • 06 699 0874
Evening wear: Via del Gesù 71a • 06 679 4634
>> www.susannalisoperletartarughe.it Open 3:30–7:30pm
Mon, 10am–7:30pm Tue–Fri, 10am–8pm Sat

Italian celebrities and genteel ladies come to Le Tartarughe's three shops for the perfect outfit for every occasion, whether it's a weekend at the beach house or a cocktail engagement. The sportswear makes creative use of superb stitching and fine fabrics, combining Jaipur silk with seersucker, for example. The evening gowns are classy and unique creations, too; some pieces, such as crimson frocks with copper straps, may seem fit for a banquet at Nero's palace, but there are also more conservative styles. Of the three stores, the main one stocks daytime clothes, the shop a few doors down has accessories – such as stylish straw totes and necklaces with artisan-blown glass beads – and the third sells evening wear and wedding dresses.

Arsenale *independent design* 6 C3
Via del Governo Vecchio 64 • 06 686 1380
Open 3:30–7:30pm Mon, 10am–7:30pm Tue–Sat

Patrizia Pieroni's temple to women's clothing has become one of the main outlets that fashionable Roman *signore* go to when looking for something truly original. From diaphanous silk dresses and exquisite shoes to spectacular necklaces and tiny clutch purses, Arsenale is Italian independent design at its best.

Marmi Line *solid marble* 6 C2
Via dei Coronari 141–5 • 06 689 3795
>> www.marmiline.com Open 10–7:30pm Mon–Sat

Hankering for a bust of Hadrian? Then pay a visit to Marmi Line, the must-visit emporium for classical statuary. It stocks a few original Roman pieces, but most of the trade is in opulent, richly coloured marble reproductions. The branch at Via dei Pastini 113 is a much more touristy and budget-friendly gift shop.

Bottega Veneta *bags of renown* `4 C3`
Piazza San Lorenzo in Lucina 11–13 • 06 6821 0024
>> www.bottegaveneta.com Open 10am–7pm Mon–Sat

The signature woven *intrecciato* pattern of Bottega Veneta's timeless leather bags is internationally recognized. But this elegant space also showcases other luxurious offerings: gorgeous shoes that mix fabrics and leather; butter-soft kid gloves; and sober outfits simply perfect for lunching and shopping.

Maga Morgana *comfort and colour* `6 C3`
Via del Governo Vecchio 27 & 98 • 06 687 9995
Open 10am–7:30pm Mon–Sat; sometimes open Sun after 4pm

Channel your inner *maga* (sorceress) at one of the area's first independent boutiques. Maga Morgana's gypsy-chic attracts Roman style-setters to two stores on the street: No. 27 has items of colourful *maglieria* (knitwear) and garments resurrected from pre-worn clothes; No. 98 stocks items by other designers.

Ferrari Store *iconic merchandise* `4 C3`
Via Tomacelli 147 • 06 689 2979
Open 10am–7:30pm daily (from 11am Sun)

You may not be able to live the lifestyle of a Formula One driver, but you can at least accessorize like one. There's something for all budgets here, from keyrings and books to scale models and branded luggage. As expected, almost everything on sale is bright red. Check out the real Formula One car at the entrance.

Pinko *for cosmo girls* `6 D4`
Via dei Giubbonari 76–7 • 06 6830 9446
>> www.pinko.it Open 10am–8pm Mon–Sat

Avant-garde yet affordable, the pieces at Pinko are for urban women with attitude. Rhinestones and laser cuts embellish their sexy tops, while the beautifully tailored trousers come in a range of neutral colours with edgy details. Pinko also has stylish-but-simple footwear and handbags to complete the look.

SBU *stylish menswear* `6 D3`
Via di San Pantaleo 68 • 06 6880 2547
Open 4–8pm Mon, 10am–1:30pm & 4–8pm Tue–Sat

Established design duo, brothers Patrizio and Cristiano Perfetti base their collections on denim emblazoned with their signature oversize zigzag stitching. Crisply tailored shirts and snakeskin belts are also available, as well as T-shirts and sweatshirts printed with cheeky slogans and graphics.

Shopping

Amomamma *sleek menswear* `6 D4`
Via dei Giubbonari 49 • 06 686 4479
Open 10am–2pm & 3:30– 7:30pm Mon–Fri (from noon Mon),
10am–7:30pm Sat, 3–7:30pm Sun

Amomamma's name is a reference to the ever-so-true stereotype of the *mammone*, the Italian man who "loves his mamma". The collections here, both smart and casual, include earth-toned, super-cool suits and funky T-shirts good for work and pleasure.

Prototype *bright young things* `6 D4`
Via dei Giubbonari 50 • 06 6830 0330   Open 3:30–8pm Mon,
10am–8pm Tue–Sat, noon–8pm Sun (not open Sun Jul & Aug)

Super-trendy Prototype offers reasonably priced casual wear for men and women. Apart from well-known international brands such as Converse, it also sells clothes by some interesting young Italian and international designers. The staff are always helpful, the shop always packed and the music always loud.

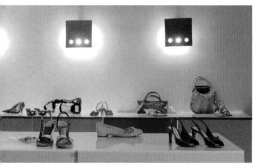

NuYorica *designer shoe store* `6 D4`
Piazza Pollarola 36–7 • 06 6889 1243
»» www.nuyorica.it   Open 10:30am–7:30pm Mon–Sat

This paradise for shoe queens stocks fun and flirty Marc Jacobs styles, L'Autre Chose kitten heels and much more. There's also a selection of designer hand-bags and women's clothes, including Balenciaga and Yohji Yamamoto. Such high style doesn't come cheap, but the sale racks out back are always worth a look.

Campo de' Fiori 52 *one-stop style* `6 D4`
Piazza del Paradiso 72 • 06 687 5775
Open 10–2pm & 4–8pm Mon–Sat

Elizabetta and Giorgio are Italian elegance personified and stock a similarly classy range of labels (including Rome's main access to Hussein Chalayan) in their small store. Great shoes, a few well-chosen accessories and their own cashmere range are also available. Don't miss their outlet store a few doors up.

empresa *fashion-forward menswear* `6 D4`
Via dei Giubbonari 25–6 • 06 683 2428
»» www.empresa.it   Open 10am–8pm daily (from noon Sun)

Men seeking some Italian style need look no further, but here it's of the edgy rather than traditional variety. Expect lesser-known but highly desirable Italian labels such as Coast, Messagerie, and their own fun and funky empresa line. There's also an interesting selection of accessories and gifts.

People *vintage bargains* `6 D4`

Piazza del Teatro Pompeo 4a • 06 687 4040 Open 3:30–8pm Mon, 10:30am–2:30pm & 3:30–8pm Tue–Sat

If vintage is what you're after, try this small store, with its height-of-cool selection of clothes and accessories from the 1960s and 70s. Alongside the affordable second-hand garments and diva-ish sunglasses are one-of-a-kind dresses, shirts, trousers and skirts designed by young owner Germana Panunzi.

Elisheva *bright shoes and accessories* `6 C4`

Via dei Baullari 19 • 06 687 1747
Open 10am–8pm Sun–Fri

Owner-designer Giorgio Moresco turns out well-priced and slightly offbeat versions of the season's hottest shoes – mainly for women, but with a few for the guys. The funky ladies' designs in this shoebox-sized shop come in brightly coloured patent leather. There's also a small selection of colourful accessories to match.

Rachele *cool for kids* `6 C4`

Vicolo del Bollo 6–7 • 06 686 4975
Open 10:30am–2pm & 3:30–7:30pm Tue–Sat

Italian style and quality aren't exclusive to adults' clothes. In a tiny, easy-to-miss street, Rachele sells handmade, colourful children's clothes, all designed in-house. Prices aren't cheap – expect to pay from 25€ for a jumper – but such well-crafted and unique kiddie couture is definitely worth the investment.

Borini *footwear to die for* `6 D5`

Via dei Pettinari 86–7 • 06 687 5670
Open 3:30–7:30pm Mon, 9am–1pm & 3:30–7:30pm Tue–Sat

If the must-have style of the season is the winkle-picker, then Borini's shelves will be lined with winkle-pickers in every combination of colour and exotic skin – from lizard to ostrich – under the sun. Borini's keen eye for fashion trends is balanced by its long tradition of quality and wearability.

Retrò *20th-century design*

6 C2

Piazza del Fico 20–21 • 06 6819 2746
>> www.retrodesign.it
Open 4–8:30pm Mon, 11am–1pm & 3:30–8pm Tue–Sat

The Bitonti sisters – Maria Pia, Adriana and Rosanna – travel the world to source the vintage pieces on sale in this stunning shop. They are passionate about their finds, and will happily talk customers and browsers through the history of any item. From Sheffield-steel teapots of the 1940s to American Bakelite jewellery and Finnish bubble chairs, this is a treasure trove of goodies for 20th-century design buffs. The furniture, ceramics, glassware, lighting and jewellery are mainly from the 1940s to the 70s, along with the odd piece of Art Deco, and include creations by the likes of Artinelli, Castiglioni, Jacobsen, Seguso, Mies van der Rohe, Aalto, Whitefriars and Murano. All are in perfect condition and artfully arranged. Prices tend to be high, but there are some affordable pieces, too, particularly among the jewellery and vase selections. This is a must-see for lovers of retro housewares and accessories, even if finances only allow for window-shopping.

Giorgi & Febbi *fabrics galore* `7 E2`
Piazza della Rotonda 61–2 • 06 679 1649
Open 10am–1pm & 4–7:30pm Mon–Fri

When the divans in the family palazzo need freshening up, look no further than Giorgi & Febbi. This old-fashioned purveyor of upholstery and fabric has been selling bolts of richly coloured brocades and intricate damasks to the local nobility since 1784. You can also pick up luxurious tassels and cushions.

Forno di Campo dei Fiori *bakery* `6 C4`
Piazza Campo dei Fiori 22 • 06 6880 6662 Open 7:30am–2:30pm & 5–8pm Mon–Fri, 7:30am–2:30pm Sat

Romans flock from far and wide for the *ricotta* cakes and *crostate di marmellata* (pastry with marmalade) sold here. But this *forno* also makes some of the best takeaway pizza in town: *pizza rossa*, with just tomato sauce, and *pizza bianca*, with olive oil. Both are light, thin and fragrant, and delicious fresh from the oven.

Campo Marzio Design *fountain pens* `4 C3`
Via di Campo Marzio 41 • 06 6880 7877
>> www.campomarziodesign.it Open 10am–1pm & 2–7pm Mon–Sat; sometimes open Sun

Dante himself would feel right at home among Campo Marzio's densely packed shelves of new (handmade) and antique fountain pens, quills and sealing waxes. The shop's signature brightly coloured, leather-bound journals are classic graduation gifts.

Galleria d'Arte Sacra *religious goods* `7 E3`
Via dei Cestari 15 • 06 678 0203
Open 9am–1pm & 3:30–6pm Mon–Fri, 9am–noon Sat

Forget the tacky souvenirs around the Vatican; this is the real deal. Here, you'll find all kinds of sacred paraphernalia, including church furniture, robes and a huge array of statues and iconography. Browsing inside without intent to buy is frowned upon by the sales assistants, but window-shopping is fine.

Angelo di Nepi *Eastern wonders* `6 D5`
Via dei Giubbonari 28 • 06 689 3006
>> www.angelodinepi.it
Open noon–7:30pm Mon, 9:30am–7:30pm Tue–Sat

Angelo di Nepi's threads are steeped in the unmistakable colours and shapes of India. Tunics with Nehru collars in rich shot silk are teamed with cropped trousers; beautifully embroidered sari fabrics are tailored into little shirts and long dresses.

GiuncArt *modern wickerware* `6 C3`
Via del Pellegrino 93 • 06 6880 6204 Open 9:30am–1:30pm
& 3:30–7:30pm Mon–Fri, 9:30am–1:30pm Sat

In a picturesque street where Roman artisans practise
their traditional crafts, Umberto Giovagnoli makes his
hand-woven straw baskets and wicker furniture right
there in the shop. Stop by to watch one of the few
preservers of this dying art at work, and maybe buy
one of his unusual, contemporary pieces.

Pasticceria Ebraica "Il Boccione" *Roman-Jewish treats* `7 F5`
Via Portico d'Ottavia 1 • 06 687 8637
Open 8am–7:30pm Sun–Thu, 8am–3:30pm Fri

Aromas of almond and cinnamon lure shoppers into this Jewish
patisserie, locally known as Forno del Ghetto – "bakery of the Ghetto" –
and famous for its small selection of mouthwatering sweet treats. Try the
ricotta cakes with chocolate or cherries, or the sweet pizza with raisins,
pine kernels and candied fruit. The service leaves a lot to be desired, but
it's the produce that brings the loyal customers back time and again.

Libreria del Viaggiatore *get travelling* `6 C3`
Via del Pellegrino 78 • 06 6880 1048
Open 4–8pm Mon, 10am–2pm & 4–8pm Tue–Sat

If Rome is but one stop on your Grand Tour, be sure to
go into this traveller's bookshop, where the shelves
are crammed floor to ceiling. Guidebooks in many
languages, maps of all sizes and to all destinations,
and a great range of *mappamondi* (globes) can't help
but stir up wanderlust in all who enter.

Bibliotea *more than just tea* `6 B3`
Via dei Banchi Vecchi 124 • 06 4543 3114 Open 3:30–8pm
Mon, 10:30am–1:30pm & 4–8pm Tue–Fri, 11am–8pm Sat

The name may be a play on words – *biblioteca* means
library – but the business of selling tea is taken very
seriously here. Check out the ceiling-high old wooden
shelves full of single-origin and blended leaf teas,
cocoa products, coffee and spices. Tea- and coffee-
making accessories, as well as books, are also sold.

Enoteca al Parlamento *wines galore* `7 E1`
Via dei Prefetti 15 • 06 687 3446
» www.enotecaalparlamento.it
Open 9:30am–2pm & 4–8:30pm Mon–Sat

Lose yourself in wineland in this wonderful *enoteca*. As well as domestic and international wines, the shop stocks balsamic vinegars (up to 80 years old), whisky and port, and all kinds of preserves. Wine is also available by the glass, served with olives and cheeses.

Modavì *styles of a bygone age* `7 E1`
Via di Campo Marzio 10c • 06 679 2520
Open 10am–7:30pm Mon–Sat; sometimes open Sun

Whether it's a present for your grandmother or a vintage-look accessory for yourself, you're sure to find something of interest among Modavì's quality, old-fashioned hats, beads, gloves and scarves. The shop's unusually tranquil atmosphere and attentive service are as much a throwback as the merchandise.

Antico Forno Roscioli *food central* `6 D5`
Via dei Giubbonari 21–2 • 06 687 5287
» www.anticofornoroscioli.com • Open 9am–8pm Mon–Sat

Once a simple, family-run *alimentari*, this swanky deli is now a self-proclaimed "taste laboratory". Few can resist the heavenly smells that emanate from the incredible array of Italian foods on offer. The tempting cornucopia includes almost 300 different types of cheese (including *strachifund*, *caciotta di bufala* and numerous cave-aged *pecorini*), some 500 wines, a large range of cured meats (such as *ciauscolo*, a soft and flavoursome salami, and *coglione di mulo*, mule's testicles), balsamic vinegars, olive oils and lots of regional specialities. Masses of home-made bakery products – among them Roscioli's delicious signature *torta di mele* (apple pie) and some kosher offerings – are sold round the corner in the Antico Forno bakery (Via dei Chiavari 34). Covering all bases, the bakery also has a swish restaurant out back and an *enoteca* that attracts a young, well-heeled evening crowd.

Brocante *collectors' heaven* `7 F2`
Via dei Pastini 15–16 • 06 679 1252
Open 11am–8pm Mon–Sat

The miniature Vespas, Ferraris and Fiats on sale in this store attract model car enthusiasts, who stock up on the latest releases. The huge array of toys, dolls and figurines draws in the kids, too. Whether tiny Testarossas or wooden Pinocchios, the stock here is Italian through and through.

Pro Fumum Durante *divine aromas* `7 F2`
Via della Colonna Antonina 27 • 06 679 5982
>> www.profumum.com Open 3:30–7:30pm Mon, 10am–7:30pm Tue–Sat (closed 1:30–3:30pm Sat)

For relief from the exhaust fumes, step into this shop for a whiff of handmade cosmetics and perfumes, as well as bath oils, eaux de toilette and candles. From florals to sultry musks, the scents here have been honed through many years of blending.

Ethic *stylish womenswear* `7 E5`
Piazza Benedetto Cairoli 11–12 • 06 6830 1063
>> www.ethic.it Open 10–8 Tue–Sat, noon–8 Sun & Mon ✓

Funky and always wearable, Ethic's clothes are a canny mix of 1960s-style femininity and current trends. Garments in lively colours and tactile fabrics, such as purple leather blazers and brocade A-line skirts, share rack space with demure silk turtlenecks and wool trousers. All come at refreshingly accessible prices.

Enoteca di Sardegna Pigna *tidbits* `7 F3`
Via della Pigna 3a • 06 678 9374
Open 10am–8pm Mon–Sat

This friendly, family-run shop sells typical Sardinian fare, from full-bodied wine and tangy *pecorino* cheese to crispy *casu* bread, *seadas* (cheese and honey pastries) and *mirto* (myrtle-berry liqueur). If you're feeling peckish, the owners will prepare a *panino* (sandwich) for you with any combination of the fillings.

Modigliani *classy gifts* `4 D2`
Via Condotti 24 • 06 678 5653
➤➤ www.modigliani.it Open 10am–2pm & 3–7:30pm Tue–Sat,
3–7:30pm Mon

This four-storey shop is a favourite with moneyed
Romans in love with their homes. Modigliani stocks
tasteful accessories, from Alessi gadgets to Murano
glassware, as well as its own lines in ceramics and
tableware. They will ship anything to anywhere.

Onyx *streetwear* `4 C3`
Via del Corso 132 • 06 6993 2211
➤➤ www.onyx.it Open 10am–8pm Mon–Sat, noon–8pm Sun

One of the better national high-street chains, Onyx
decks out aspiring pop princesses with sunny casuals
and bright tracksuits of typical Italian quality, at
pocket-friendly prices. Although some of the clothes
are definitely for the young of body, the practical
shoulder bags and gorgeous sunglasses appeal to all.

Michel Harem *a magnificent mishmash* `5 E3`
Via Sistina 137a • 06 474 6466
Open 10am–9pm Tue–Sat, 3–9pm Sun & Mon

This emporium stocks outlandish reproductions, old
treasures and unique antiques – from a fake stuffed
lion's head to life-size angels. Eccentric owner Michel
– a hairdresser and minor morning-TV celebrity –
scours flea markets and antiques dealers around the
world to find the curios that he loves to sell.

Mandarina Duck *practical bags* `4 D3`
Via dei Due Macelli 59 • 06 678 6414
➤➤ www.mandarinaduck.com Open 10am–7:30
Tue–Sat, 3:30–7:30pm Mon

The affordable handbags, travel bags, duffels and
totes at MD are loved for their clean lines and modern
materials – such as their patented Mitrix (a 3-D hybrid
of synthetics). The products are functional and hip,
and distinctive for their lack of ornamentation.

High Fashion
Rome may not be Milan, but it does offer branches
of nearly all the big-name designers, and their
gorgeous boutiques make it tempting to swipe the
plastic. The principal designer thoroughfare is Via
Condotti, home to **Gucci, Prada, Dolce & Gabbana**
(the couture line), **Ferragamo, Bulgari** for jewellery
(see p62), **Armani, Alberta Ferretti** and **Valentino**.

Via Borgognona runs parallel and counts **Fendi,
Ermenegildo Zegna, Moschino** and **Versace** mens-
wear among its tenants; **Versace** womenswear and
fellow Italian couture boutique **Mariella Burani** are
on the cross-street Via Bocca di Leone. On Piazza
di Spagna itself are **D & G** (the streetwear line),
Missoni, Sergio Rossi and **Frette** for de-luxe lin-
ens. For further details, *see p180*.

Shopping

Shopping for Antiques

The city's antiques shops are clustered on certain streets. Pedestrianized **Via dei Coronari** – lined with medieval, Renaissance and Baroque buildings – is the main thoroughfare. It is packed with over 40 dealers selling anything from furniture to statues from all eras. It is an expensive road to shop on, but then the quality is high. Twice a year, Via dei Coronari plays hosts to an antiques fair, the **Fiera dell'Antiquariato**, when market stalls line the carpeted street; the first is in mid-May, the second in mid-October. Other good streets for browsing are **Via dell'Orso** and **Via dei Soldati** (just off Coronari), as well as **Via del Babuino** and **Via Giulia**. If buying antiques, make sure the dealer provides export documentation. Many shops will ship goods abroad.

Fausto Santini *shoes and bags* `5 D3`

Via Frattina 120 • 06 678 4144

» www.faustosantini.com Open 11am–7:30pm Mon, 10am–7:30pm Tue–Sat, noon–7pm Sun

Rome's Fausto Santini left a career in law to become a shoemaker. His handmade, butter-soft leather shoes for women and men are stylish and supremely comfortable. The bags are often quirky yet timeless; some are designed especially to match the footwear.

TAD *lifestyle concept store* `4 C2`

Via del Babuino 155a • 06 3269 5125

» www.taditaly.com Open 10:30am–7:30pm Mon–Sat (from noon Mon, to 8pm Sat), noon–8pm Sun (Jun–Sep: closed Sun)

Step into TAD for the lowdown on what's hot in Rome. Everything has a price tag in this one-off department store, so you can buy it all, from the fixtures and fittings to ultra-cool clothes by international designers such as Alexander McQueen and Hussein Chalayan.

Bulgari *all that glitters is gold* `4 D2`

Via Condotti 10 • 06 679 3876

» www.bulgari.com Open 3–7pm Mon, 10am–7pm Tue–Sat

Bulgari's fabulously glitzy jewellery has a timeless luxury about it. This *fin de siècle* store is where founder Sotirio Bulgari started out in 1898. That 195-carat necklace Nicole Kidman wore to the 2004 Oscars may be beyond your budget, but there might be something in your range among the jewellery, watches and glasses.

Simona *update your undies* `4 C2`
Via del Corso 82–3 • 06 361 3742
Open 10am–7:30pm Mon–Sat (from 11am Mon)

This tiny shop has one of the widest selections of lingerie and swimwear around. Leave your modesty at the door, as the shop girls here often barge into your dressing room. From high-end brands such as Dolce & Gabbana *(see p61)* to La Perla's cheaper Occhiverdi line, Simona has something for everyone.

Buccellati *big, beautiful jewellery* `4 D2`
Via Condotti 31 • 06 679 0329
>> www.federicobuccellati.it Open 3:15–7pm Mon, 10am–1:30pm & 3–7pm Tue–Fri, 10am–6pm Sat

Gold pendants dripping with globs of diamonds, rubies and emeralds typify the outrageously glamorous pieces at Buccellati, one of Italy's most venerable goldsmiths. Unashamedly baroque, the designs here have been a favourite of jet-setters for decades.

Cravatterie Nazionali *tie the knot* `4 C2`
Via Vittoria 62 • 06 6992 2143
Open 3:30–7:30pm Mon, 9:30am–7:30pm Tue–Sat

This sleek, compact shop carries elegant ties, cravats, bow ties and scarves by all the most important Italian designers – from Armani to Versace – as well as foreign *haute couture* houses such as Dior. Should you require assistance, the friendly and attentive staff will even show you how to tie the perfect knot *all'italiana*.

Nostalgica *vintage footie gear* `4 C2`
Via di Ripetta 30–31 • 06 321 9448
Open 2–8pm Mon, 10am–8pm Tue–Sat, 11am–8pm Sun

Specialist store Nostalgica sells brand-new soccer shirts modelled on original designs – from the early 1900s to the 1980s – from almost every European football team. Popular sellers include strips from the former Soviet and East German teams. Old newspaper cuttings of momentous matches line the walls.

Shopping

Schostal *retail restraint* `4 C3`
Via del Corso 158 • 06 679 1240
Open 9:30am–7:30pm Mon–Sat, 10:30am–7pm Sun

Since 1870 Schostal has been providing sensible shirts and no-frills accessories to discerning customers. Now one of the few remaining old-style retailers in the Via del Corso – worth visiting for its original fittings alone – this is the place to find a set of initialled handkerchiefs or that smart office tie.

Luisella Mariotti *delicate jewellery* `4 C2`
Via di Gesù e Maria 20a • 06 320 1320
≫ www.luisellamariotti.com

Open 10:30am–7:30pm Mon–Sat (from 2:30pm Mon)

Young Italian designer Luisella Mariotti and her assistant make intricate and elaborate jewellery from precious and semi-precious stones, enamel, glass and copper. You can even watch them working in the back of the shop. The price tags are reasonable.

Yamamay *good-value underwear* `4 C3`
Via Frattina 86 • 06 6919 0260
≫ www.yamamay.com Open 10–8 Tue–Sat, 11–8 Sun & Mon

Named after a Japanese silkworm, Yamamay offers simple, classy, comfortable and affordable nightwear, bras and knickers. Their styles are a refreshing departure from the other, typically froufrou Italian lingerie brands, and their swimwear creations come in bright, young colours and interesting textures.

Emporio Libreria 'Gusto *cook's corner* `4 C2`
Piazza Augusto Imperatore 7 • 06 323 6363
≫ www.gusto.it Open 10.30am–10pm daily

Part of the 'Gusto triumvirate of gourmet restaurants next door *(see p35)*, this little shop inside a Fascist-era palazzo stocks a pleasing array of kitchen gadgets and homewares. White porcelain dishes and aluminium trollies are among the many sleek and functional finds here, along with cookbooks in Italian and English.

Libreria Francesco Ponti *old books* `4 C3`
Via Tomacelli 23 • 06 6880 8203 Open 4–7:30pm Mon, 9:30am–1pm & 4–7:30pm Tue–Sat (closed Sat Jun–Sep)

This friendly little bookshop is reminiscent of a bygone era, with its precarious stacks of antique and second-hand books, from junk-sale paperbacks to precious first editions from as far back as the 18th century. For a polyglot clientele, there are titles in Italian, German, French, English and Spanish.

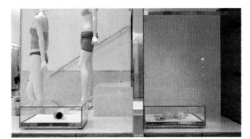

La Perla *lingerie at its most luxurious* `4 D2`
Via Condotti 79 • 06 6994 1934
>> www.laperla.com Open 3–7pm Mon, 10am–7pm Tue–Sat

Welcome to the world of the 80€ thong. On entering this seductive and plush flagship of Italy's best lingerie house, you'll soon fall for the gorgeous feminine garments and simple-but-sensual designs – all in classic blacks, greys, creams and whites. Prices may be high at La Perla, but then so is the wow factor.

Alinari *images of the past* `4 D2`
Via Alibert 16a • 06 679 2923
>> www.alinari.it Open 3–7pm Mon, 9am–1pm & 3–7pm Tue–Sat
(closed Sat & open from 9am Mon Jun–Sep)

Known for its historic scenes of Italian cities, including many of Rome, Florence-based Alinari is Italy's oldest and most famous photography firm. You can buy coffee-table books and prints, as well as lampshades, trays and other objects printed with the countless evocative images taken from the original glass negatives in the archive. Prints range from 25€ to 300€.

Buccone *traditional wine shop* `4 C2`
Via di Ripetta 19 • 06 361 2154
Open 9am–8:30pm Mon–Thu, 9am–midnight Fri & Sat

A charming wine shop with old ads on the walls, Buccone has been selling wines from all over Italy – as well as liquors from around the world – since 1870. It's also a good spot for some wine tasting, or for a simple, hearty meal: roasted meats, stews and pasta are served for lunch (Mon–Sat) and dinner (Fri & Sat only).

High-Street and Budget Shopping

For shopping that's easy on the pocket, head to Via del Corso, Via Cola di Rienzo (loved by locals), Via Nazionale (the most traffic-heavy of the bunch) or cobblestoned Via dei Giubbonari. You'll find all the usual suspects – **Benetton**, **Sisley** and **Stefanel**. They aren't exactly dirt-cheap, but the quality is good. At shops such as **Avant**, **Brooks** (for men) and **Sportstaff**, low-priced ultra-trendy garments fly off the racks and can make for some fun, guilt-free spending. For cheap footwear, a few shops at the top of Via Nazionale fit the bill. Rome's department stores, including **La Rinascente** and **COIN**, are underwhelming, but useful for the basics. For rock-bottom prices, though, check out **MAS**, where hardly anything is above 10€. For further details, *see p180–81*.

Shopping

Francesco Biasia *the bag man* 4 D3
Via Due Macelli 62–62a • 06 679 2727
>> www.biasia.com
Open 1:30–7:30pm Mon, 10am–7:30pm Tue–Sat

Edgy, practical and affordable, Biasia's bags have it all. In mainly solid hues, with stylish detailing, the specialities are roomy shoulder bags in leather, canvas or plastic. They are internationally renowned, but the best selection, at the best prices, is still here in Italy.

Xandrine *glamorous evening wear* 4 C2
Via della Croce 88 • 06 678 6201
Open 10:30am–7:30pm Mon, 9:30am–7:30pm Tue–Sat

You can pretend to be Cinderella at this old-fashioned boutique, where fairy-godmother sales assistants will fit you with dreamy evening gowns and wedding dresses off the peg or made to order. The glittering garments have a high-end look and feel that belie their surprisingly modest price tags.

Abitart *chic and unique* 4 C2
Via della Croce 46–7 • 06 6992 4077
>> www.abitartworld.com
Open 10:30am–8pm daily

The clothes at Abitart ("dress art") are a skilful mix of baroque styling, bright colours and modern materials. The results are one of a kind, though not too daring to wear. The collections are designed for grown-up ladies, but drenched in the rainbow palette of kids' clothes.

Il Discount dell'Alta Moda *sales city* 4 C2
Via di Gesù e Maria 14–16a • 06 361 3796
Open 2:30–7:30pm Mon, 10am–7:30pm Tue–Sat

These no-frills outlets (one for men, one for women) offer bona-fide Italian high-fashion designers at up to 80 per cent off normal retail prices. There are some truly great deals to be had – whether it's an Armani suit or a Gucci bag, Prada shoes or a Versace top – as long as you don't mind last season's stock.

OCCASIONI SPECIALI

Pulp *a fashion retrospective* `5 E5`

Via del Boschetto 140 • 06 485 511

Open 4–8pm Mon, 10am–1pm & 4–8pm Tue–Sat

This boutique is a great source for modish and well-priced women's vintage clothing. From funky patterned shirts to cool coats and flowery dresses, the clothes and retro jewellery are sure to get you noticed. The shop staff often modify the clothes, embellishing old garments with flowers and appliqué.

LOL *couture and culture* `5 F5`

Piazza degli Zingari 11 • 06 481 4160

Open 10am–8pm Mon–Sat (closed for lunch in summer)

The racks are already filled with unusual clothes and far-out silver jewellery, but this boutique-cum-gallery still finds room to support local artists, putting on regular exhibitions of young and unknown painters and sculptors. Members of Rome's artistic community are among those who favour this shop.

Le Gallinelle *theatrical threads* `5 E4`

Via del Boschetto 76 • 06 488 1017

>> www.legallinelle.it

Open 3:30–8pm Mon, 10am–1pm & 3:30–8pm Tue–Sat

New and second-hand clothes, from the dramatic to the classic, are sold here. Owner Wilma's pricey selection is a strange but successful mix of styles, with textiles from around the world and covetable accessories. She also makes costumes for theatre and film.

Produce Markets

For a slice of true Roman life, find the nearest fruit-and-vegetable *mercato* – every neighborhood has one and they're usually open 7am–2pm Mon–Sat. **Piazza Testaccio**'s (Map 8 D3) lively covered market, where women in housedresses and bedroom slippers shuffle through, tut-tutting at the rising cost of courgettes, is one of the most authentic in the city. Trastevere's **Piazza San Cosimato** (Map 8 C2) has become a bit touristy, and the famous **Campo dei Fiori** (Map 6 D4) now sells as many junky trinkets as vegetables, but both still provide local *trattorie* with fresh produce. Due to its gentrified location near the Vatican, the covered **Piazza dell'Unità** (Map 1 C2) is more expensive than most, but then again, the basil leaves always seem a bit perkier here.

Shopping

Maurizio de Nisi   *retro homewares*   `5 E4`
Via Panisperna 51 • 06 474 0732
Open 4–7:30pm Mon, 10am–1pm & 4–7:30pm Tue–Sat

Maurizio scours the country for the 20th-century Italian furniture, lamps and home accessories on sale here. His mother Anna runs the shop, her passion for what she sells shining through in her discussions with clients. From 1920s bars to 1970s wooden chairs, all the merchandise is in excellent condition.

La Vetrata di Passagrilli   *arty glass*   `5 E5`
Via del Boschetto 94 • 06 474 7022
» www.ivetridipassagrilli.it
Open 10am–2pm & 3–8pm Mon–Fri, 10am–2pm Sat

Passagrilli makes glass objects unlike any you've seen before. His unique technique – *vetro-fusione* (glass fusion) – consists of "cooking" various sheets of coloured glass together. Apart from unusual lamps and jewellery, he also makes wall hangings.

Soul Food   *for vinyl junkies*   `9 H1`
Via di San Giovanni in Laterano 192–4 • 06 7045 2025
» www.haterecords.com
Open 10:30am–1:30pm & 3:30–8pm Tue–Sat

Vinyl buffs will have a field day rummaging through rare Italian and import LPs and singles at this brightly painted shop. Don't expect many bargains, though. Soul Food also sells CDs and other indie record-store fare – cool gadgets, fanzines, posters and books.

Trimani Enoteca   *established wine shop*   `5 G2`
Via Goito 20 • 06 446 9661
» www.trimani.com   Open 9–1:30 & 3:30–8 Mon–Sat 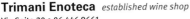

The Trimani family has been in the wine business since 1821, and their current emporium is larger than most Roman supermarkets. The brothers who run the place travel throughout Italy in search of interesting wines and emerging labels. They'll gladly recommend a bottle or two if you specify your price range and taste.

Panella, L'Arte del Pane *fine bakery* `5 G5`
Largo Leopardi 2 • 06 487 2344 Open 8am–1:30pm & 5–8pm
Mon–Wed, Fri & Sat, 8am–1:30pm Thu, 8:30am–1:30pm Sun

As its name suggests, this amazing patisserie and
bread shop raises baking to an art form. Apart from
torte rustiche (savoury pies) of every kind, bread and
breadsticks, Panella churns out delicious cakes (not as
dry as some Italian confections) and unbelievably rich
sweets and pralines, and sells pulses, flours and wine.

Disfunzioni Musicali *the DJ's choice*
Via degli Etruschi 4 • 06 446 1984 • Bus Nos. 71, 204, 492
» www.disfu.com Open 3–8pm Mon, 10:30am–8pm Tue–Sat

Established and aspiring DJs flock to this mecca for
new and second-hand British and US techno, electronica and indie labels. In the heart of the university
quarter, this is also a good place to come for the news
on upcoming club nights, as the walls both inside and
out are plastered with promo flyers and posters.

Fiorucci *labels, labels and more labels* `5 F3`
Via Nazionale 236 • 06 488 3175
Open 11:30am–8pm Mon, 9:30am–8pm Tue–Sat

No brand is as emblematic of 1980s Italian fashion as
Fiorucci, with its flashes of hot pink and lace and signature pouting cherubs. In addition to the house label,
modified to look less Cyndi Lauper and more Britney
Spears, the shop also sells other hot young brands,
such as Miss Sixty, Killah and Moschino Cheap & Chic.

Goodfellas *music central*
Circonvallazione Casilina 44 • 06 4544 9836 • Train to Lodi
» www.goodfellas.it Open 10:30am–7:30pm Mon–Sat

In an ugly but arty area, this record store is where the
serious DJs go. Small but incredibly well stocked, with
rare Italian labels as well as all the latest imports of
electronica, hip-hop, rock, rock steady, ska, soul and
funk, Goodfellas is also the outlet store for the fast-
growing independent label of the same name.

Volpetti *fantastic foodstore* 8 D3
Via Marmorata 47 • 06 574 2352
>> www.volpetti.com
Open 8am–2pm & 5–8:15pm Mon, 8am–8:15pm Tue–Sat

Volpetti has one of the most incredible selections of cheese (both fresh and seasoned) and cold meats you will ever see, as well as high-class caviars and pâtés. The jovial men behind the counter will gladly let you sample anything before you buy.

Officina della Carta *handmade paper* 8 C1
Via Benedetta 26b • 06 589 5557
Open 9:30am–1pm & 4–7:30pm Mon–Sat

This old-fashioned paper workshop in the heart of Trastevere makes and sells its beautifully bound photo albums, diaries and binders in a range of styles and materials, all hand-crafted to perfection. Customized orders, with your choice of cover, paper and size, can be ready in just a few days.

Libreria del Cinema *for film buffs* 8 C1
Via dei Fienaroli 31d • 06 581 7724
>> www.libreiadelcinema.roma.it Open 5–9pm Mon, 11am–9pm Tue–Thu, 11am–midnight Sat, 11am–9pm Sun

Set up by 11 prominent names in italian cinema, this stylish bookshop sells publications on everything from Hollywood directors to European arthouse cinema, as well as a superb range of CDs and DVDs. Its organized events, exhibitions and trendy bar add to its appeal.

Other Good Bookshops

Apart from the national chains, the best bookshops in Rome take some hunting down. For purely English-language titles, two shops merit visits: the **Lion Bookshop** has been serving expats for decades, and the **Anglo-American Book Co** has top-notch art and architecture titles. **Ta Matete** stocks beautiful but expensive coffee-table art books. **Feltrinelli International** has plenty of fiction, nonfiction, plays and poetry in English and Spanish, and a few titles in other languages. Cosier alternatives – with mainly Italian titles – are **Fahrenheit 451** (for cinema), **Amore e Psiche** (for philosophy and psychology) and **Odradek** (for comics). Lovingly selected second-hand books can found at **La Diagonale**. For further details, *see p179–80.*

Enoteca Ferrara *the essential ingredient* `8 C1`
Via del Moro 1 • 06 5833 3920
Open 8pm–1:30am daily

Hardly more than a counter and a window display, tiny Ferrara sells top-notch regional delicacies from olive oil to dried tomatoes, pasta to preserves. It's only open in the evening, so if you want to shop during the day, nip into the restaurant round the corner and ask them to open up for you – they'll be more than willing.

Joseph Debach *one-of-a-kind shoes* `8 C1`
Vicolo del Cinque 19 • 06 580 6633
>> www.josephdebach.com Open evenings only; call for times

Tooled metallic leather mules with toes that curl up like elves' shoes are among the eye-popping works of art at Joseph Debach. Incorporating strange materials, such as cobblestones and old newspapers, each pair is unique. Some are more wearable than others, but that's not the point: this is art.

Benedetto Franchi *food in all its finery* `4 A2`
Via Cola di Rienzo 200–204 • 06 686 4576
>> www.franchi.it Open 8:15am–8pm Mon–Sat

This temple to Italian foodstuffs near the Vatican sells hams, salamis, cheeses, mozzarellas and a huge range of delicacies, including some 100€ truffles. A city institution since 1925, Franchi also attracts quite a lunch crowd with its hot take-out food. Their *supplì* (fried rice balls filled with cheese) are the best in town.

Bibli *a veritable warehouse of books* `8 C1`
Via dei Fienaroli 28 • 06 588 4097
>> www.bibli.it Open 11am–midnight daily (from 5:30pm Mon)

In a vine-covered alley in Trastevere, multilevel Bibli has an extensive, carefully selected stock (mainly Italian), including many scholarly tomes. Frequent book launches, signings, readings and discussions are held in a specially dedicated space. Bibli also has a good community bulletin board and a relaxing café.

art & architecture

More than any other city in the world, Rome is a living museum, where archaeological ruins sit comfortably under and alongside spectacular architecture from all eras. Art is everywhere – and much of it can be enjoyed for free – from ancient artifacts on show in post-industrial spaces to awe-inspiring Renaissance frescoes in their original ecclesiastical settings.

ART AND ARCHITECTURE

The glories of Imperial and papal Rome are enough to keep any visitor engaged for weeks, but the artistic and architectural offerings of the city go deeper than ancient ruins and Baroque churches. In the *centro storico* and beyond, a wide range of world-class sights represent some of the greatest artists in history and provide fascinating insights into Rome's chequered past and modern evolution. Best of all, much of it can be enjoyed for free.

Sylvie Hogg

The Roman World

Time has softened Rome's Imperial splendour, but ruins like the Colosseum *(see p12)* and Roman Forum *(see p89)* still dominate the skyline and are testaments to the West's greatest civilization. In the Musei Capitolini *(see p88)*, the marble busts of Roman citizens are among less formidible but no less impressive Roman remains.

Great Basilicas

Consecrated in the 4th and 5th centuries and embellished over the years, the city's most monumental churches are treasure troves of religious relics and art. St Peter's *(see p12)* is the undisputed king, San Giovanni in Laterano *(see p93)* is Rome's one true cathedral, and Santa Maria Maggiore *(see p93)* is filled with dazzling mosaics.

The Baroque Outdoors

In the 17th century, an explosion of papal patronage and a few key architects transformed the city, giving Rome its theatrical piazzas, sinuous lines and playful fountains. Piazza Navona *(see p125)* and the Spanish Steps *(see p81)* are high Baroque perfection, while the Fontana di Trevi's *(see p15)* over-the-top decoration prefigures Rococo excess.

choice sights

Art Museums

Large-scale hoarding of ancient and Renaissance art has given Rome some of the world's most outstanding museums. The **Vatican Museums** *(see p94)* and the **Musei Capitolini** *(see p88)* contain an incredible collection of masterpieces, while the intimate **Galleria Borghese** *(see p84)* is home to stunning Baroque works.

Fascist Creations

Roman architecture in the 1920s and 30s was political rhetoric, copying the forms and materials of Imperial monuments to propagate ideas of "Fascist empire". The southern suburb of **EUR** *(see p91)* has the best examples, but see also the **Piazza Augusto Imperatore** (Map 4 C2), and the **Foro Italico** complex around the Stadio Olimpico *(see p101)*.

21st-Century City

Projects headed by top international architects have given modern architecture a convincing presence in Rome. Check out Zaha Hadid's daring **MAXXI** *(see p83)*, Richard Meier's **Ara Pacis Museum** *(see p81)* – the first new construction in the *centro storico* since the 1930s – and Renzo Piano's striking **Auditorium Parco della Musica** *(see p102)*.

Art & Architecture

Palazzo Altemps *classical statuary* `6 D1`

Piazza Sant'Apollinare 48 • 06 3996 7700
>> www.archeorm.arti.beniculturali.it
Open 9am–7:45pm Tue–Sun

Housed in a fabulously restored 15th-century palazzo, this collection of classical artifacts forms part of the Museo Nazionale Romano *(see p86)*. Exhibits include the 5th-century BC Ludovisi throne, with its carved bathing nymphs, and a statue of a thuggish Hercules. **Adm**

Sant'Agnese in Agone *Baroque church* `6 D2`

Piazza Navona • 06 6819 2134
Open 8am–noon & 4–6pm Tue–Sun

Not content to play wallflower to Bernini's exquisite fountain in the centre of the square, Borromini gave the piazza this show-stopping church, endowing a medieval original with a towering façade and dome that bow and flex with Baroque curvature. The theatrical exterior belies an interior of modest proportions.

Santa Maria della Pace *war and peace* `6 C2`

Vicolo dell'Arco della Pace 5 • 06 686 1156
>> www.chiostrodelbramante.it
Open 10am–12:45pm Tue–Fri; cloisters open 4–8pm daily, later at weekends

This pretty church was commissioned in the 15th century by Sixtus IV to honour the peace *(pace)* achieved between the Romans and the Florentines. Adorning the interior is Raphael's famous *Sibyls* fresco. The 16th-century cloisters, the **Chiostro del Bramante**, are among the city's finest. They now house exhibitions of contemporary art.

Sightseeing Discount Cards

Many of Rome's best sights are free, but those that do charge can be expensive. If you plan to visit lots of places, it's worth buying a discount card from PIT tourist offices. The seven-day **Roma Archeologica Card** (20€) covers ten sights, including the Colosseum and the Palatine; the seven-day **Museum Card** (9€) covers the entrance to the five Museo Nazionale Romano branches. The **Roma Pass** (18€) offers three days of public transport, free entry to two sights or museums and reduced prices into other sights and museums. The annual **Go.Card** (6€), for 18–30-year-olds, offers large discounts on sights, cinemas, bars and shops (www.gocard.org). All museums are free to EU citizens under 18 and over 65 years of age.

Museo di Roma *Roman treasure-trove* `6 D3`
Palazzo Braschi Via di San Pantaleo 10 • 06 6710 8346
>> www.museodiroma.comune.roma.it Open 9am–7pm Tue–Sun

Items used in Roman daily life from the Middle Ages onwards are shown in this 18th-century palazzo, which includes rooms reconstructed from demolished mansions. Intricate 17th-century cityscapes painted by Luigi Vanvitelli hang alongside clothes, portraits and furniture belonging to the great papal families. **Adm**

Santa Maria Sopra Minerva `7 F3`
Piazza della Minerva • 06 679 3926
Open 7am–7:15pm daily

Rome's only Gothic church was built in the 13th century on top of an earlier one, which had itself been built over a Roman temple to Minerva. It boasts frescoes by Filippino Lippi and a statue of Christ by Michelangelo. Bernini carved one of the tombs and a bust, as well as the elephant holding the obelisk in the piazza outside.

Pantheon *temple to all gods* `7 E2`
Piazza della Rotonda • 06 6830 0230
Open 8:30am–7:30pm Mon–Sat, 9am–6pm Sun

Built by Hadrian in AD 118 on the same spot as the original 27 BC Pantheon and consecrated as a church in AD 609, this is Rome's best-preserved ancient building. The massive, elegant interior is lit by a a 9-m (30-ft) hole in the dome. Highlights are the original bronze doors and marble floor, and Raphael's tomb.

Raphael in Rome

In 1508, when Bramante suggested that Raphael (1483–1520) help redecorate the Vatican apartments, Pope Julius II was so impressed by his sketches for the Stanza della Segnatura that he dismissed all the other artists. The frescoes in two of the three rooms, with elegant compositions and harmonious use of colour, were executed by the master himself; the others by his assistants. His frescoes include the Prophet Isaiah in **Sant'Agostino** *(see p182)* and the sea nymphs at the **Villa Farnesina** *(see p87)*. Raphael's portraits of Renaissance bigwigs hang in the **Galleria Doria Pamphilj** *(see p79)* and the **Galleria Borghese** *(see p84)*, while **Palazzo Barberini** *(see p84)* is home to *La Fornarina*, a portrait of his bare-breasted lover.

Art & Architecture

Il Gesù *Baroque model* `7 F4`
Piazza del Gesù • 06 697 001
Open 6am–12:30pm & 4–7:15pm daily

This monumental shrine to the Counter-Reformation is the principal church of the Jesuits in Rome. Built between 1568 and 1575 by Giacomo Vignola and Giacomo della Porta, it inspired Baroque architecture the world over. Il Baciccia's *Triumph of the Name of Jesus* ceiling-fresco reveals remarkable foreshortening.

Museo Crypta Balbi *medieval traces* `7 F4`
Via delle Botteghe Oscure 31 • 06 3996 7700
>> www.archeorm.arti.beniculturali.it
Open 9am–7:45pm Tue–Sun

Part of the Museo Nazionale Romano *(see p86)*, this beautifully designed museum shows the social and architectural evolution of Rome from ancient times to the present day. Walkways also take you through excavations of the ancient Teatro di Balbo. **Adm**

Galleria Doria Pamphilj *art gallery* `7 G3`
Palazzo Doria, Piazza del Collegio Romano 2 • 06 679 7323
>> www.doriapamphilj.it Open 10am–5pm Fri–Wed

Still owned by the Doria Pamphilj family (the present prince lives upstairs), this superb palazzo contains works by Breughel, Poussin, Correggio and Bernini. The Velázquez painting of Pope Innocent X, a Pamphilj ancestor, is outstanding. When shown the painting, the pope exclaimed "You have seen too much". **Adm**

Bernini in Rome
Rome's curvaceous architecture and sensual statues are largely thanks to Gian Lorenzo Bernini (1598–1680), the driving force behind Italian Baroque. As pet architect and sculptor to the popes of the time, Bernini received many church commissions. In **St Peter's** *(see p94)*, he designed the bronze baldachin that towers over the main altar, as well as the colonnade outside. Bernini's talent lay in translating human emotions into stone, as seen in the angels' faces on **Ponte Sant'Angelo** *(see p15)*. In one of his most impressive sculptures, The *Ecstasy of Santa Teresa* (**Santa Maria della Vittoria**; *see p182*), the saint's expression of religious rapture recalls passion of a different kind. *Beata Ludovica Albertoni* (**San Francesco a Ripa**; *see p182*) also has erotic overtones.

Caravaggio in Rome

The grim realism of Michelangelo Merisi da Caravaggio (1571–1610) revolutionized European art forever. Over 25 of his paintings and altarpieces can still be seen in Rome. **San Luigi dei Francesci** *(see p182)* houses the compelling *Life of St Matthew*. His *Madonna di Loreto* (**Sant'Agostino**, *see p182*) depicts Mary as a peasant girl and faithfully portrays destitute pilgrims. The focal point of the *Conversion of St Paul* (**Santa Maria del Popolo**, *see p82*) is the unlikely rear of a horse. To realistically render the spurting blood in *Judith Beheading Holofernes* (**Palazzo Barberini**, *see p84*), Caravaggio attended Beatrice Cenci's public execution. Beheading was a frequent theme and the **Galleria Borghese** *(see p84)* is home to the grisly *David with the Head of Goliath*.

Galleria Spada *fine art and whimsical architecture*   6 D5
Palazzo Spada Piazza Capo di Ferro • 06 687 4893
>> www.galleriaborghese.it Open 8:30am–7:30pm Tue–Sun

This jumble of paintings was lovingly re-collected after being dispersed in World War II. Highlights include works by Rubens and Jan Breughel. It's worth the entrance fee just for the architectural joke of Borromini's trompe l'oeil marble corridor in the courtyard garden. By a trick of perspective, the corridor appears to be three times its actual length and ends with a statue that looks life-size but is actually no bigger than a garden gnome. **Adm**

Area Sacra di Largo Argentina   7 E4
These four Roman temples, dating from as early as the 3rd century BC, were discovered when the area was cleared for re-building in 1926. You get a good feel for the place by wandering its street-level periphery, but to get up close and personal, you'll need to get a permit *(see p23 for details)*. Try not to trip over any of the stray cats that are cared for by the feline sanctuary in the same piazza (www.romancats.com).

Sant'Andrea della Valle *operatic church*   6 D4
Corso Vittorio Emanuele II 6 • 06 686 1339
Open 7:30am–noon & 4:30–7:30pm daily

The first act of Puccini's *Tosca* is set in this mammoth Baroque church. Inside are copies of Michelangelo's statues of Leah – who represents the active life – and Rachel – the contemplative life. The "talking" statue Abate Luigi is outside: Romans used to cover it with subversive notes during the papal reign.

Art & Architecture

Isola Tiberina *romantic river island* 8 D1

The only island in the Tiber is linked to the Ghetto on the east bank by Ponte Fabricio (built in 62 BC), Rome's oldest surviving bridge. In 289 BC, the island became a shrine to Aesculapius, the god of healing, after a snake (the god's animal form) allegedly washed up here and ended a plague. Home to a working hospital, Isola Tiberina still retains its medical links.

In the 1st century BC, engineers shored up Isola Tiberina into the shape of a ship. From the lower walkway (water level permitting), a travertine fragment of the ship's "hull" is still discernible off the port bow. Where the temple to Aesculapius used to stand, there is now the 10th-century San Bartolomeo church (rarely open; *see p182*); an inscription across its portico states that the saint's body lies inside. On the island's southern tip are the rustic remains of Rome's earliest stone bridge (built in the 2nd century BC), now called Ponte Rotto ("broken bridge"), while to the west is the Ponte Cestio (46 BC; rebuilt in 1892), which leads to Trastevere.

Via del Corso *retail artery* 4 C3

One of Rome's first streets, now a major shopping hub with elegant covered arcades, Via del Corso was once part of the Via Flaminia. Its new name came from the riderless horse race first held here in 1466. During the papal reign (AD 496–1870), this long stretch was the city's festival street. German writer J W Goethe described Carnevale here as a drunken debauch of cross-dressing and masks, where "everyone has leave to be as mad and foolish as he likes". Since decadent popes no longer rule Rome, nothing as exciting happens today. Halfway down the street, the extraordinary 42-m (137-ft) Column of Marcus Aurelius *(see p183)* stands in Piazza Colonna; it was raised around AD 180 to celebrate the Emperor's victory over the Germanic tribes. The statue of St Paul on the top was added in the 1500s. Dominating the square's north side is the imposing Palazzo Chigi *(see p184)*, built for the Chigi family of bankers-turned-popes, now the official residence of the prime minister and closed to the public.

Ara Pacis *reassembled monument* `4 C2`
Via di Ripetta, Lungotevere in Augusta • 06 6710 3887
Open 9am–7pm Tue–Sun

Erected in 9 BC to commemorate the peace Augustus
had secured in the Empire, the Altar of Peace disap-
peared in the mists of time. Under Mussolini, its dispersed fragments were tracked down and rebuilt. A
new glass enclosure, designed by American architect
Richard Meier, has been built to house the altar. **Adm**

Piazza di Spagna and the `4 D2`
Spanish Steps *cosmopolitan Rome*
The bright and breezy, palm tree-lined Piazza di
Spagna is so named because it contains the Spanish
Embassy. The square used to be the haunt of English
milords and other rich north Europeans. Today, the
characters may have changed, but the famous square
is still a magnet for foreign visitors.

   The iconic Spanish Steps *(see p184)*, sweeping up
from the east side of the piazza, provide respite for
weary souls who bask in the sun, write postcards or
just observe the pageant below. The steps are packed
day and night, so come early in the morning to fully
appreciate the beauty of the space. The curving tiers
of the staircase – actually built by the French in 1725
– lead up to the magnficent twin-towered Trinità dei
Monti church *(see p183)*, which commands one of the
best views in Rome. At the foot of the steps is the boat-
shaped Fontana della Barcaccia, a fountain designed
in 1629 by Bernini's less famous father, Pietro.

Keats-Shelley Memorial House `4 D2`
Piazza di Spagna 26 • 06 678 4235
≫ www.keats-shelley-house.org
Open 9am–1pm & 3–6pm Mon–Fri, 11am–2pm & 3–6pm Sat

Romantic poet John Keats was only 25 when he died
of TB here. The house was preserved as a memorial
and library to honour him and his English contempo-
raries Shelley and Byron. Exhibits include paintings,
books, manuscripts and other memorabilia. **Adm**

Art & Architecture

Piazza del Popolo *gateway to the city* 4 C1

Dramatic, open and grandiose, Piazza del Popolo forms the base of a trident, whose prongs are the three straight roads leading south into the heart of Rome. The square is a fantastic example of how almost everything in Rome is the result of centuries of architectural tinkering.

The stone gate at the northern end is where the old Roman Via Flaminia reached the capital – throughout the centuries of papal rule, this was most foreigners' first sight of the city. Pope after pope competed with his predecessors to make the entrance ever more impressive. Originally known as Porta Flaminia, the gate was revamped in 1562 to a Michelangelo design and renamed Porta del Popolo for Pius IV. At the behest of Alexander VII, further embellishments were carried out by Bernini in the 1650s. On either side of the gate are the city walls that Emperor Aurelian built to defend Rome from barbarians in the 3rd century AD. To the east of the gate is Santa Maria del Popolo (see p183), not much to look at from the outside, but housing quite a treasure-trove of art inside, including Caravaggio's *Conversion of St Paul* and *Crucifixion of St Peter*, and Raphael and Bernini's Chigi chapel. This spot is also where Emperor Nero was allegedly buried after his murder.

Today, the gate opens on to the vast oval public space of the piazza, which has a pink granite obelisk at its centre. The obelisk, with its bold hieroglyphics, was brought from Egypt by Emperor Augustus.

On the square's south side is a pair of what appear to be twin churches – Santa Maria dei Miracoli (see p182) and Santa Maria in Montesanto (see p183) – built in the 17th century by architect Carlo Rainaldi. Space limitations dictated that the churches be different sizes, but the illusion of similarity is achieved by one having a round dome and the other an oval one. During Carnevale, the popes would treat the public to executions and tortures in the piazza; nothing so extreme happens now – just rock concerts and political rallies.

MACRO *contemporary art* `5 G1`

MACRO: Via Reggio Emilia 54 Open 9am–7pm Tue–Sun
Il Mattatoio: Piazza Orazio Giustianiani 4
Open 4pm–midnight Tue–Sun
>> www.macro.roma.museum • 06 6710 70400

Rome may not be renowned for its contemporary art scene, but for those bored of emperors and popes, the Museo d'Arte Contemporanea di Roma (MACRO) will come as a breath of fresh air. The two gallery buildings here are arguably more noteworthy than the art itself: the main site is a conversion of an early 20th-century brewery, which is home to an interesting permanent exhibition of Italian art since the 1960s, including a fabulous flaming column by Masbedo. It also hosts temporary exhibitions. Its aim, when complete, is to showcase both performance art and installations alongside contemporary painting and sculpture. The second locations, Il Mattatoio, is housed in the city's former slaughterhouse (1881–91) and is only open for temporary exhibitions. **Adm**

Museo Hendrik Christian Andersen *weird statuary* `4 B1`
Via Pasquale Stanislao Mancini 20 • 06 321 9089
Open 9am–7pm Tue–Sun

This bizarre museum houses the completely unerotic nudes sculpted by Hendrik Christian Andersen, boy-friend of author Henry James. Andersen built this pseudo-palazzo and moved in with his mother, immortalizing her face in ceramic plaques in the façade.

MAXXI *art in the new millennium* `2 B2`
Via Guido Reni 10 • 06 321 0181
Open 11am–7pm Tue–Sun

These former barracks will be home to the Museo Nazionale delle Arti del XXI Secolo – of 21st-century art – when Anglo-Iraqi architect Zaha Hadid finishes transforming them. At present, temporary exhibitions are held in a nearby hangar. Shows have included work by Ed Ruscha, Isaac Julien and Kara Walker.

Galleria Borghese *Rome's finest gallery* `3 F5`

Villa Borghese • 06 32 810
>> www.galleriaborghese.it
Open 9am–7pm Tue–Sun (booking essential)

This intimate gallery is studded with masterpiece after breathtaking masterpiece. Cardinal Scipione Borghese built the gallery in 1613 to showcase his superb art collection, most of which is still intact. The magnificently frescoed ground floor houses ancient Roman mosaics – including some gory gladiator scenes – as well as sculptures (many copies of Greek originals). Bernini (1598–1680) is the real star of the show, however, with works such as the heart-stopping *Apollo and Daphne* and his gripping self-portrait as David. Various busts portray the gallery's patron, while the more unusual sculpture by Antonio Canova depicts Napoleon's sister Paolina as a topless Venus. Paintings include Raphael's *Lady with a Unicorn* and Titian's lyrical *Sacred and Profane Love*. The 2-hour audio tour is worth the money. **Adm**

Piazza Barberini *old Rome meets new* `5 E3`

This square is where old Rome ends and new Rome begins. Buildings are taller, streets are wider and insurance companies supplant the quaint *trattorie* and shops of the *centro storico*. Despite the snarl of traffic, Bernini's two fountains still play. Carved for Pope Urban VIII in the 1640s, they are decorated with the Barberini family insignia of bees. On one corner of the square stands the church of Santa Maria della Concezione *(see p182)*, the crypt of which holds the artfully arranged bones of Capuchin monks in separate chapels: one for skulls, another for pelvises, and so on. Across the square, Palazzo Barberini (designed by Bernini and rival Borromini) displays the eclectic canvases of the Galleria Nazionale d'Arte Antica (National Gallery; *see p183*), including Raphael's racy *La Fornarina (see p77)* and Caravaggio's *Judith Beheading Holofernes (see p79)*. Rather suprisingly amid all the Italian Old Masters, Holbein's famous *Henry VIII* makes an incongruous appearance. **Adm**

Palazzo del Quirinale & Scuderie del Quirinale `5 E4`
presidential palace

Palazzo del Quirinale: Piazza Montecavallo • 06 46 991
>> www.quirinale.it Open Sep–Jun 8:30am–noon Sun
Scuderie del Quirinale: Via XXIV Maggio 16 • 06 696 270
>> www.scuderiequirinale.it Open 10am–8pm daily
(to 10:30pm Fri & Sat)

The pink Palazzo del Quirinale, on top of the highest of Rome's seven hills, was built in the 16th century as the papal summer residence. Il Quirinale has housed various kings of Italy, but these days it is the Italian president's official residence. Inside, there's a stunning collection of tapestries and some delightful gardens. Just across the square are the Scuderie, the former papal stables, refitted in the late 1990s to host major travelling art exhibitions. On the piazza outside are an obelisk from the Mausoleum of Augustus and a Dioscuri fountain, with 5.5m- (18ft-) tall figures of Castor and Pollux. Classical concerts are held every Sunday at noon in the pretty Cappella Paolina. **Adm**

Via del Quirinale Churches *Baroque jewel boxes* `5 E3`

San Carlo alle Quattro Fontane: Open 10am–1pm & 3–6pm Mon–Fri, 10am–1pm Sat, noon–1pm & 3–6 pm Sun
Sant'Andrea al Quirinale: Open 8am–noon & 4–7pm Wed–Mon

These neighbouring Baroque churches typify the stylistic contrast between rival architects Borromini and Bernini. At Borromini's tiny San Carlo (1631–41) – his first and favourite church – alternating concave and convex walls create a palpable tension. Bernini's Sant'Andrea, begun in 1658, is also small, but coloured marble, cherubs and gilded stucco impart a feeling of grandeur.

Contemporary Art

Surrounded by the Villa Borghese park, Rome's most important collection of late 19th-century and 20th-century European art is held at the **Galleria Nazionale d'Arte Moderna** *(see p183)*. Much of the work is by relatively unknown Italians, but there are some works by Surrealist De Chirico and Futurist Giacomo Balla, as well as international artists such as Cézanne, Kandinsky and Pollock. Rome's contemporary-art scene has long been ridiculed, but the **British School** *(see p183)* and the **Academie Française** *(see p183)* at the Villa Medici both mount good temporary exhibitions, as does **MACRO** *(see p83)*. A new museum of 21st-century art, **MAXXI** *(see p83)*, will house the best compendium of contemporary international works in the city.

Fontana di Trevi *iconic fountain* `7 G1`

Hackneyed photo-op for the coach-tour set it may be, but this Baroque mammoth of a fountain in Piazza di Trevi is nevertheless an amazing sight. The entire structure, an 18th-century pageant of mythology in marble, seems to rise from a single piece of travertine at the fountain's base. Teeming with coin-hurling tourist life much of the time, the Trevi is most glorious – and most peaceful – before breakfast or after midnight.

Museo Nazionale Romano `5 G3`

Palazzo Massimo alle Terme: Largo di Villa Peretti 1
06 3996 7700 Open 9am–7:45pm Tue–Sun
>> www.archeorm.arti.beniculturali.it

Home to most of the antiquities found in Rome since 1870, this museum now has five branches: Palazzo Massimo; the Aula Ottagonale *(p183)*; Terme di Diocleziano *(p183)*; Palazzo Altemps *(p76)*; Museo Crypta Balbi *(p78)*. The restored Palazzo Massimo has the most impressive holdings, with frescoes, mosaics, architectural fragments and sculpture from the vast state collection of ancient Roman art, among which is a bronze sleeping *Hermaphrodite* and a Roman copy of Praxiteles's *Aphrodite of Cyrene*. Upstairs is a magnificent reconstruction of a Roman dining room; the original walls, with frescoes, were excavated from the villa belonging to Livia, wife of the first Roman emperor, Augustus. These walls could no doubt tell some tales, since she allegedly poisoned her husband's heirs so her own son Tiberius could inherit the Empire. **Adm**

The Fountains of Rome

Fountains gurgle, trickle, jet and cascade in every corner of Rome. A bit of a cliché, but undeniably impressive, is the **Fontana di Trevi** *(see above)*. In Bernini's **Quattro Fiumi** in Piazza Navona *(see p125)*, four river gods personify the Nile, Ganges, Danube and Plate, symbolizing the geographical reach of the Church over four continents. In the Ghetto area is the exquisite **Tartarughe** fountain, originally built in the 1580s by Giacomo della Porta and Taddeo Landini. In 1638, Bernini gave the fountain its namesake turtles. In antiquity, 13 aqueducts brought 38 million gallons of water to Rome each day from springs in the countryside; drink some today from the spouts of the many functional nasone (big-nose) fountains, which are dotted all over the city.

Domus Aurea *Nero's golden house*   `9 G1`
Via della Domus Aurea • 06 3996 7700
>> www.archeorm.arti.beniculturali.it
Open 9am–7:45pm Wed–Mon (booking essential)

In AD 65, after allegedly setting fire to Rome, Nero built himself a palace and park that covered one-third of the city. Known as the Golden House, this vast, partially preserved residence, now underground, has halls with wonderful frescoes and original fake stalactites. **Adm**

Basilica di San Clemente *layers of religion*   `9 G1`
Via San Giovanni in Laterano • 06 774 0021
Open 9am–12:30pm (from 10am Sun) & 3–6pm daily

Few places show the layering of Rome's architecture as well as San Clemente. Here, a 12th-century church, San Clemente, is built on top of a 4th-century one, which in turn sits above a temple to the Persian god Mithras, who was popular with Roman soldiers and whose namesake religion rivalled Christianity in Imperial times. An underground river trickles audibly through the lower excavations, where work continues. **Adm**

Teatro di Marcello *ancient playhouse*   `8 D1`
Via del Teatro di Marcello • 06 6710 3819
Open 9am–6pm daily

This huge theatre, built in 13 BC, once seated 15,000. After the Orsini family used it as a fortress in the Middle Ages, the building was converted into a residence; some lucky Romans still live here today. Inside is off-limits, but you can wander around the outside and see the arches that inspired the Colosseum.

City of Frescoes
In ancient Rome, frescoes, rich in natural motifs, were used to embellish domestic spaces – there are fine examples in the **Museo Nazionale Romano** *(see p86)*. In medieval times, the Church used frescoes to promote religious conversion, as seen in the 13th-century **Santi Quattro Coronati** *(see p183)*. Conversely, at **Santo Stefano Rotondo** *(see p183)*, 16th-century frescoes of gruesome martyrdoms were designed to discourage Catholics from converting to Protestantism. During the Renaissance, frescoes reflected the indulgence of their patrons; the ceiling of the **Villa Farnesina** *(see p77)* depicts orgiastic scenes of naked ladies and gods from Ovid's *Metamorphoses*. Frescoes could also be illusionistic: the "dome" in **Sant'Ignazio** *(see p182)* is actually a fresco.

Art & Architecture

Campidoglio & Musei Capitolini 7 G5

Musei Capitolini: Piazza del Campidoglio • 06 3996 7800
>> www.museicapitolini.org Open 9am–8pm Tue–Sun

The primordial spur of tufa rock at the north end of the Roman Forum is the Campidoglio, or Capitoline, the most sacred of Rome's seven hills and centre of religious and political life in ancient Rome. Its summit was home to the huge temple of the Romans' chief god, Jupiter Capitolinus; today only a few blocks remain. The Palazzo Senatorio, present-day Rome's town hall, now presides over a Michelangelo-designed square, flanked by the two palazzos that form the Musei Capitolini. At the piazza's centre is a copy of the 2nd-century bronze statue of Marcus Aurelius; the more impressive original is in the museum. The museum also houses the sculpture of the *Dying Gaul* – a fallen soldier who was originally thought to be a gladiator – as well as many fine ancient bronzes, including the famous *She-Wolf* (a 5th-century-BC Etruscan piece). Upstairs are paintings by Caravaggio and Tintoretto. **Adm**

Case Romane di Santi Giovanni e Paolo 9 G2
a window on ancient Rome

Clivo di Scauro • 06 7045 4544
>> www.caseromane.it Open 10am–1pm & 3–6pm Thu–Mon

A well-kept secret, this cluster of ancient Roman buildings lies under the church of Santi Giovanni e Paolo. Originally incorporating shops and a block of flats, the complex was converted in the 3rd century AD into a grand family home with unusual frescoes. **Adm**

Sport in Imperial Rome

For ancient Romans, the vicious spectacles that often resulted in death were the equivalent of a spectator sport. The 65,000-capacity **Colosseum** (Map 9 F2) staged gladiator and animal fights, and chariot races were held at the 300,000-seat **Circus Maximus** (Map 9 E2). These events were free and held year-round. Successful gladiators and charioteers were the superstars of their day and many a wealthy Roman lady would pay to sleep with them. Less popular, due to the absence of violence, were the Greek-style athletics competitions at the Stadium of Domitian (where Piazza Navona now stands). Members of the public exercised at public baths such as the **Terme di Caracalla** (Map 9 G3), partaking in a bit of sparring with a trainer.

Ancient Rome *Rome's foundations* `9 E1`

Roman Forum: enter from Via Sacra, Largo Romolo e Remo or Via del Foro Romano Open 9am–1hr before sunset daily
Trajan's Markets: Via IV Novembre • 06 679 0048 Open 9am–1hr before sunset Tue–Sun
Palatine: Via di San Gregorio 30 • 06 3996 7700 Open 9am–1hr before sunset daily

The Capitoline hill may have been the political and religious nerve centre of ancient Rome, but it was the Roman Forum and its Imperial neighbours that were the true heart of the city for over 1,000 years.

The **Roman Forum** stretches from the Arch of Titus (near the Colosseum) to the Campidoglio. After the fall of Rome in 476 AD, the valley was used as a cattle pasture and it became buried under a layer of dirt, rubble and cow dung. Archaeological excavations began at the end of the 19th century and now the ruins, ranging from 1,400 to 2,500 years in age, can be explored.

Near the Arch of Titus stands the Basilica of Maxentius and Constantine, the law courts of ancient Rome; Michelangelo copied its arches for St Peter's. Further in is the round Temple of Vesta, where the six Vestal Virgins tended the Eternal Flame of Rome. The Vestals took vows of chastity before they were ten years of age, and lived by them for 30 years; if the vows were broken, the virgins were buried alive. Next door, the House of the Vestal Virgins, with its flowered garden, is one of the prettiest parts of the Forum.

Close by lies an open space where political meetings were held and criminals executed. Here you'll find the Rostra, the platform from which politicians would address the crowd. This is where Mark Antony made his "Friends, Romans and Countrymen" speech over Caesar's body, after which the mob burned their hero on the spot where the Temple of Divus Julius stands. Fresh flowers mark the location. The nearby Mamertine Prison is where St Peter was allegedly detained.

Across the Via dei Fori Imperiali are the Imperial Forums, which contain **Trajan's Markets**, a massive ancient shopping and office complex.

On the west side of the Roman Forum is the **Palatine** hill. During Imperial times, this was *the* place for the city's rich and powerful to reside. The first emperor, Augustus, lived modestly up here, but his successors all built grand residences – today only traces remain. Green and flower-filled in spring, the Palatine is the most pleasant of the city's ancient sites to wander. **Adm** (to Palatine and Imperial Forum only)

Piazza della Bocca della Verità 9 E1

Santa Maria in Cosmedin: **06 678 1419**
Open 9am–1pm & 3pm–6pm daily
San Giorgio in Velabro: **06 6920 4534**
Open 10am–12:20pm & 4–6:30pm daily

The chaotic roundabout that forms this piazza was
once the ancient Roman cattle market, Forum Boarium.
Set amid oleanders and umbrella pines beside the
river, two temples from this period still stand. The
round one is dedicated to Hercules, protector of
cattlemen; and the small but perfectly rectangular
one to Portunus, the god of harbour activities.
Opposite is the church of **Santa Maria in Cosmedin**,
with its fine Romanesque bell tower that features
prominently on the city's skyline. The Mouth of Truth
carving in its portico – which is said to bite the hands
of liars – draws hordes of tourists. Just north of here,
down a quiet street leading to the Forum, is the
8th-century **San Giorgio in Velabro**, with wonderful
14th-century frescoes and a restored Ionic portico.

Piazza dei Cavalieri di Malta *vista* 8 D3

Priorito di Malta: 3 Piazza dei Cavalieri di Malta
06 6758 1234 Open 9am–1hr before sunset daily

The walled villa here is the sovereign territory of the
Knights of Malta, an anachronistic Christian order
with its own head of state and embassies. But it's
Piranesi's fanciful square outside that's the real draw
– look through the keyhole in the priory gate to see
the most extraordinary view of St Peter's Basilica.

Michelangelo in Rome

Renaissance genius Michelangelo Buonarroti (1475–
1564) is most famous for his **Sistine Chapel**
frescoes *(see p94)*, but he actually preferred the
subtractive art of sculpture and believed that each
chunk of Carrara marble had a soul waiting to be
released. His 1498 *Pietà* in **St Peter's** *(see p94)* is
an exquisite early masterpiece. The tomb of Julius II,
in **San Pietro in Vincoli** *(see p183)*, with its fine
sculptures of Moses, Leah and Rachel, was to be
his crowning glory. Sadly, financial troubles meant
the project fell far short of the artist's original
ambitions. An architectural visionary, Michelangelo
also gave Rome the soaring dome of St Peter's, the
façade of **Palazzo Farnese** *(see p184)*, and the sunny
and stately **Piazza del Campidoglio** *(see p88)*.

Santa Sabina *early Christian basilica* `8 D2`
Via Santa Sabina • 06 5794 0600
Open 6:30am–12:45pm & 3:30–7pm daily

The simplicity of Santa Sabina (AD 422) makes a refreshing change from the Baroque styling of many of the city's churches. Its three naves, columned arcades and high windows were inspired by the Basilica of Maxentius and Constantine *(see p89)*. Highlights are the original wooden doors and the leafy cloisters.

EUR *Fascist grandeur*
Museo della Civiltà Romana: Piazza Giovanni Agnelli 10
06 592 6041 • Ⓜ **EUR Palasport or EUR Fermi**
Open 9am–6pm Tue–Sun

The district of EUR (Esposizione Universale di Roma), started by Mussolini in 1938 and situated far south of the centre, is an intriguing showcase of Fascist (or Rationalist) architecture. The buildings, coordinated initially by architect Marcello Piacentini, were inspired by ancient Rome, but the aesthetic is colder and more severe, with impersonal travertine façades of a size to match Il Duce's ego. Construction was interrupted by World War II and, despite the fall of the Fascist regime, building resumed in the 1950s, though on a smaller scale than originally planned. Several museums offer the chance to look inside the buildings, including the Museo della Civiltà Romana, with its fascinating 1:250 scale model of 4th-century AD Rome. Also worthwhile is an up-close visit to the massive Palazzo della Civiltàdel Lavoro, known as the "square Colosseum".

Holy Relics
From miscellaneous body parts to instruments of torture used in martyrdoms, Rome brims with relics. The authenticity of some is questionable, but believe and you will be rewarded with incomparable sights. Pieces of the True Cross and the Crown of Thorns can be seen in **Santa Croce** *(see p182)*. The **Scala Santa** *(see p183)*, a staircase from Pontius Pilate's house in Jerusalem, was moved to Rome by Emperor Constantine's mother Helena. St Peter's shackles are in **San Pietro in Vincoli** *(see p183)*; John the Baptist's head is in **San Silvestro in Capite** *(see p183)*; the grill on which St Lawrence was barbecued is in **San Lorenzo in Lucina** *(see p182)*; and an arrow that shot St Sebastian is in the church above his namesake **catacombs** *(see p95)* on Via Appia Antica.

Art & Architecture

Centrale Montemartini *ancient relics* 10 B4
Via Ostiense 106 • 06 574 8030
>> www.centralemontemartini.org Open 9:30am–7pm Tue–Sun

Luminous marble Venuses and temple pediments are set against a backdrop of cold iron machinery and industrial catwalks in this stunning museum, which is set in a former power station. The classical statuary is the overspill from the Musei Capitolini's *(see p88)* huge collection. There are a bookshop and a café. **Adm**

Santa Cecilia *place of martyrdom* 8 D2
Piazza Santa Cecilia • 06 589 9289
>> www.basilicasantacecilia.it
Church and excavations open 9:30am–noon & 4–7pm daily; fresco open 10am–11:30pm Mon–Sat, 11:30am–noon Sun

This church was once the house of the patron saint of music; you can see the steam room where the Roman authorities tried to scald Cecilia to death. The adjoining convent houses a superb 13th-century fresco. **Adm**

Santa Maria in Trastevere *mosaics* 8 C1

Piazza Santa Maria in Trastevere • 06 581 4802
Open 7:30am–9pm daily

Built in the 4th century to replace a Roman soldiers' drinking den, this wonderful basilica was the first church ever to be dedicated to the Virgin Mary. The Romanesque bell tower noisily chimes the quarter-hours all day and night, while the façade has a superb, if fading, 12th-century mosaic of the Madonna.

Inside, the 22 granite columns were looted from the Baths of Caracalla. The 12th-century inlaid marble floor is also recycled from ancient Rome, with bits of marble rearranged into swirls and starbursts by the crafty Cosmati family, whose designs inspired pavements in many churches. The 13th-century mosaics in the apse are exquisite, with Christ and the Evangelists all aglitter in gold and coloured tiles. The church was restored in the late 18th century by Prince Henry Stuart (brother of Bonnie Prince Charlie), who was brought up in Rome and whose coat of arms is above the door.

Via della Lungara *sight-studded street* **1 D5**
Palazzo Corsini: No. 10 • 06 6880 2323
Open 8:30am–1:15pm Tue–Sat, 8:30am–1:15pm Sun
Villa Farnesina: No. 230 • 06 683 883 Open 9am–1pm Mon–Sat

From the Porta Settimiana, Via della Lungara leads from Trastevere to the Vatican – about a 15-minute walk. The road passes the Orto Botanico *(see p135)*, in the former gardens of Palazzo Corsini. Originally built in the 15th century and remodelled in the 18th, the palace was home to the lesbian exile Queen Christina of Sweden; the room in which she died has not been touched since her death in 1689. The palazzo is now part of the Galleria Nazionale d'Arte Antica, housing works by Rubens, Van Dyck and Titian. Across the road is the 16th-century Villa Farnesina, built by Agostino Chigi, patron of Raphael, whose Galatea frescoes of sea nymphs *(see p87)* adorn the walls. During banquets at the villa, Chigi would hurl silver plates into the Tiber; unbeknown to his guests, he hid nets under the water and retrieved everything once they had gone. **Adm**

Tempietto del Bramante *architectural masterpiece* **8 B1**
Piazza San Pietro in Montorio • 06 581 3940
Open 9:30am–12:30pm & 4–6pm (winter 2–4pm) Tue–Sun

This sublime little Doric rotunda in a hidden courtyard, perched high on the Gianicolo hill, was the first modern building to follow exact Classical proportions. Designed by Donato Bramante, it was commissioned in 1499 by Queen Isabella of Spain to mark the spot where she thought (wrongly) St Peter had been crucified. These days, it's commonly held that his martyrdom actually took place just north of here, where the Vatican now stands.

A Pilgrimage to the Seven Basilicas

In 1299, a rumour started that if you went to Rome the next year, your sins would be forgiven and you would go to heaven. Pope Boniface VIII thought it such a good idea that he decreed 1300 a Holy Year, to attract pilgrims from all over Europe. Catholic jubilees are now held every 25 years. To qualify for salvation, you must visit all seven of the official pilgrimage churches in the Holy Year: **San Giovanni in Laterano** (Rome's cathedral and central church of the Catholic world); **Santa Maria Maggiore**; **San Paolo Fuori le Mura** (where the Apostle was executed); **St Peter's** *(see p94)*; **Santa Croce in Gerusalemme**; **San Lorenzo fuori le Mura**; and **San Sebastiano**. Unfortunately, you'll now have to wait until 2025. For further details, *see pp182–3*.

Art & Architecture

Città del Vaticano *the Catholic State* 1 B3

St Peter's Basilica: Open Apr–Sep: 7am–7pm daily; Oct–Mar: 7am–6pm daily (dome open 8am–1hr before closing)
Tours of Necropolis & St Peter's Tomb: Details and booking on 06 6988 5318 (book as far in advance as possible)
Vatican Museums: 06 6988 3333 Open 8:45am–4:45pm Mon–Fri, 8:45am–1:45pm Sat and last Sun of the Month; Nov–Feb: 8:45am–1:45pm Mon–Sat; check website for details.
>> mv.vatican.va

With its own postal system, web domain (.va) and police force (the striped and plumed Swiss Guard), the Vatican City is a fully fledged independent state. The site of the Vatican owes its holiness to the fact that St Peter was crucified here in AD 64 and supposedly buried under what is now St Peter's Basilica. Spine-tingling guided tours of the excavated necropolis beneath the church point out the alleged tomb. With a dome 132 m (436 ft) high, the church looms larger than anything the Apostle could ever have imagined; it is one of the biggest churches in the world. To give an idea of the scale, each blue-on-gold mosaic letter of the Latin inscription in the nave is 2 m (6 ft 6 ins)

tall. In front of the church, the vast ellipse of Piazza San Pietro is embraced by Bernini's colonnade. The broad and bombastic Via della Conciliazione, leading from the piazza, was built by Mussolini in 1929.

A ten-minute walk east of St Peter's lies the entrance to the Vatican Museums. Don't miss the Octagonal Courtyard, with such superb statues as the stoic *Apollo Belvedere* and the heart-rending *Laocoön*. Also of note is the collection of modern religious art, with works by artists such as Paul Klee, Henry Moore and Picasso. At the end of the museums are the Raphael Rooms and the Sistine Chapel, where Michelangelo's meaty ceiling frescoes inspire awe and neck aches.

Papal audiences, open to all, are held every Wednesday; pick up a ticket on Tuesday afternoon from the Swiss Guards' post located between St Peter's Square and the Basilica (on the square's north side). The pope blesses the crowds in the square from his window every Sunday at noon. Both the Vatican and St Peter's have a strict dress code: no bare shoulders or knees for women; men must wear long trousers. **Adm**

Castel Sant'Angelo *formidable fortress* `1 D3`
Lungotevere Castello 50 • 06 681 9111
>> www.galleriaborghese.it Open 9am–7:30pm Tue–Sun

From opulent Renaissance apartments to the pope's
escape route from the Vatican, this labyrinthine
museum covers all aspects of the building's history.
Begun as a mausoleum by Hadrian in AD 128, it later
evolved into a fortress, prison and papal residence.
Views from the battlements are breathtaking. **Adm**

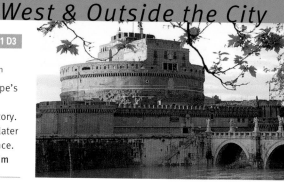

Catacombe di San Sebastiano *tombs*
Via Appia Antica 136 • 06 785 0350 • Bus Nos. 118, 218, 660
>> www.catacombe.roma.it
Open 8:30am–noon & 2:30–5pm Mon–Sat

Frequent 30-minute guided tours take you through a
maze of hand-dug tunnels, Christian and pagan
tombs, and underground churches. Fourth-century
mosaics, Greek inscriptions and paintings adorn the
catacomb walls, which cover some 8 km (5 miles). **Adm**

Ostia Antica *ruined sea port*
Viale dei Romagnoli 117 • 06 5635 8099 • Train to Ostia Antica
Open 8:30am–7pm Tue–Sun (Nov–Mar: 8:30am–5pm)

Rome's ancient port may not be as well preserved as
Pompeii or Herculaneum, but it is still in remarkable
condition. Wandering the ruins, you get a real taste of
life under the Empire. Theatres, bars, shops, public
baths and even the firemen's quarters can all still be
seen. It's thought that malaria was the cause of the
city's decline, killing thousands and forcing the rest
of the population – which is estimated to have topped
100,000 – to flee. Spot the differences between the
apartment blocks that housed the masses and the
luxurious detached mansions of the rich few; and take
a look at the many religious buildings – temples, a
synagogue and a basilica – to see how the various
faiths lived happily side by side. Few crowds and lax
custodians make for adventurous, intimate exploring.
Frequent trains from Porta San Paolo railway station
take about 30 minutes to reach Ostia Antica. **Adm**

>> *Apply in advance for papal audiences by faxing the Prefettura della Casa Pontificia on 06 6988 5378*

performance

From dance performances held in intimate venues to the football matches at the grandiose Stadio Olimpico, there's much in Rome to delight lovers of live events. Among its unique attractions are live gigs in *centri sociali* squats and classical music concerts in the strikingly modern Parco della Musica. The city really comes alive, though, in summer, when festivals of all types take place in the open air.

PERFORMANCE

It might take a little digging to find them, but Rome has cultural distractions in abundance. Be prepared for a late start, though, as events often don't get going until close to midnight. In summer, the city unveils its full artistic glory when shows move outside to make the most of the balmy nights. From open-air opera at the Termi di Caracalla to late, wild nights in lively clubs and underground events in the *centri sociali*, Rome always offers an element of surprise.

Gerard Hutching

Classical Music and Opera

Acoustically stunning and a work of art in itself, Renzo Piano's **Auditorium Parco della Musica** *(see p102)* has become *the* place to hear classical music in Rome, while opera's home is the plush **Teatro dell' Opera di Roma** *(see p104)*. In summer, the ruins of the **Terme di Caracalla** *(see p88)* serve as a backdrop for the both types of performance.

Theatre and Dance

Rome has more theatres than any other city in Italy, ranging from the highly respected **Teatro Ghione** *(see p107)* to the reliably excellent (and stunningly scenic) **Teatro Valle** *(see p101)* and **Teatro Argentina** *(see p100)*, where classical ballet is also sometimes performed. The **Teatro dell'Opera di Roma** *(see p104)* is an important dance venue, too.

Blues and Jazz

The Eternal City has an undying love for blues and jazz. **Big Mama** *(see p107)* is the city's legendary home of the blues, while leading jazz venue **Alexanderplatz** *(see p106)* is just one of a dozen great jazz clubs, which include **La Palma** *(see p103)*. A recent addition, the sleek **Casa del Jazz** *(see p103)* attracts top international artists.

choice acts

Centri Sociali

Uniquely Roman, these alternative venues have their collective fingers on the pulse of the latest artistic happenings. Most are non-profit-making and occupy old buildings. One of the largest, **Villagio Globale** *(see p104)*, hosts concerts, plays and films. **Rialto Sant'Ambrogio** *(see p132)* focuses more on jazz and experimental music and theatre.

Cutting-Edge Performance

For avant-garde events and theatre with a difference, check out **Teatro Palladium** *(see p105)*, **Teatro Vascello** *(see p107)* and former soap factory **Teatro India** *(see p107)*. Each stages experimental and multi-disciplinary pieces. *Centri sociali* such as **Forte Prenestino** *(see p99)* and **Acrobax Project** *(see p99)* schedule more of the same.

Rock and Pop Concerts

During the summer, the city often hosts events where international and national pop stars headline *(see pp16–17)*. Big names also play venues such as the **Auditorium Parco della Musica** *(see p102)* and the **Stadio Olimpico** *(see p101)*. Up-and-coming talent is best seen at **Classico Village** *(see p105)*, and the *centri sociali*.

Performance

Modo *live music*

6 C2

Vicolo del Fico 3 • 06 6867 7452
>> www.modo.roma.it Check website for opening times

Fresh on the scene, popular Modo is a centrally located club and bar offering a mix of live Nujazz, bossa nova and visiting DJs. Local, national and international names such as Joseph Malik, Jazid and the Kyoto Jazz Massive play. The venue's cool interior is matched by an equally cool crowd.

Teatro Argentina *centre for the arts*

7 E4

Largo di Torre Argentina 52 • 06 6840 00346
>> www.teatrodiroma.net Box office open 10am–2pm & 3–7:15pm Mon–Sat, and from 8pm on performance days

Rome's main theatre, "l'Argentina", opened in 1732. Its glorious frescoed ceiling dates from that time, but the current façade was added 100 years later. Rossini's *Barber of Seville* premiered here, though it was much disliked, and only later gained popularity and acclaim. Today's varied programme – a high-quality mix of experimental and classical theatre, opera, dance and poetry events – is usually well received. The most innovative acts are shown in October and November during the RomaEuropa Festival *(see p18)*, when international companies bring plays and dance shows to the city. Catching a performance in such beautiful, plush surroundings is an experience theatre-lovers shouldn't miss. The venue also has a *centro studi* (library) of posters, screenplays, bills, photos and videos of performances held at the theatre since 1964. It's open to the public by appointment (call 06 6840 0050).

Cinema Teatro-Farnese `6 D4`

Piazza Campo di Fiori 56 • 06 686 4395
>> www.teatrodiroma.net

After a lengthy restoration, cult cinema Teatro-Farnese reopened in 2006. Its heydey was in the 1960s and 70s when it was a meeting place for intellectuals. Today, it shows a variety of mainstream and art-house films in their original language, and holds cinema-related exhibitions in the foyer.

A Roman Summer

In summer, outdoor locations come alive with festivals and events, from the charmingly lit Palatino to Capocotta beach's free parties. For all kinds of events, including outdoor theatre, cinema, music festivals and fairs held by political parties, see listings on www.gayroma.it, and in *Zero 6*, *Trovaroma* and *Roma C'é*.

Teatro Valle *grand and glorious* `7 E3`

Via del Teatro Valle 21 • 06 6880 3794
>> www.teatrovalle.it
Box office open 10am–7pm Tue–Sat, 10am–1pm Sun

Some of the country's most interesting modern theatre companies – including Raffaello Sanzio, as well as Italian acting legend Tommaso Salvini – have performed at this stunning 18th-century venue. The theatre also stages music concerts – from Portuguese fado to rock opera and recitals – and, very occasionally, dance performances.

Stadio Olimpico *top football*

Via Foro Italico • 06 36 851 • Ⓜ Flaminia, then
Bus No. 25 Ticket office times vary by event; call for details

Rome's two teams, AS Roma (www.asromacalcio.it) and SS Lazio (www.sslazio.it), both in Serie A, share this grandiose Mussolini-era stadium, playing at home on weekends from September to May. Midweek UEFA Cup and Champions League matches are also held here, as are international games.

Stadio Flaminio *Italian rugby union* `2 A1`

Viale Tiziano • 06 3685 7845
Ticket office times vary by event; call for details

When not being used for lower-league football, this 24,970-seat stadium, built for the 1960 Olympics, is home to the national rugby team (which plays in the Six Nations Championships). Tickets are available from Italy's Rugby Federation (www.federugby.it) and also several banks – see www.air.it to locate one.

Performance

Auditorium Parco della Musica
2 C2
contemporary musical amphitheatres
Via Pietro de Coubertin 15 • 06 8024 1281
≫ www.auditoriumroma.com Box office open 11am–6pm daily, and from 8pm to the start of each show on performance days

Opened in 2002 after years of delays, the Auditorium Parco della Musica is the long-awaited major space for music and culture that Rome always lacked, and the new home to the prestigious Santa Cecilia music academy. Its three main halls, the biggest of which has capacity for 2,800 people, feature classical music, as well as jazz, pop and rock concerts. The cherry wood-lined walls make for excellent acoustics. In the middle of the huge complex – which also houses a book and CD shop, a bar, a trendy restaurant and the remains of

an ancient Roman villa – there is a 3,000-seat open-air arena, called the Cavea, which stages world-music, blues and jazz concerts in summer. The auditorium's innovative architect, Italian star Renzo Piano, has also created the landscaped park linking the complex with MAXXI *(see p83)*, the nearby centre for contemporary art. Living up to expectation, the Auditorium is fast becoming Rome's cultural hub, attracting performers like Patti Smith, Norah Jones and Cecilia Bartoli. Major political events have also been hosted here. Guided tours of the complex – including a look at the Roman villa and artifacts found during excavations of the site – take place every hour (10:30am–5:30pm Sat & Sun and public holidays; call 06 8024 1281 for information and bookings). Also *see p126*.

Teatro Ambra Jovinelli *comedy nights*
5 H5
Via Guglielmo Pepe 43–7 • 06 4434 0262
≫ www.ambrajovinelli.com Box office open 10am–7pm Tue–Sat, 11am–2pm Sun (closed Aug)

The spiritual home of Italy's socially engaged comedians and satirists has been going since 1909. Ambra Jovinelli has hosted some of Italy's best-known comic actors over the years, including Totò and Paolo Rossi. Jazz is also sometimes featured.

La Palma *loud and varied*
Via Giuseppe Mirri 35 • 06 4359 9029 • Ⓜ Tiburtina
>> www.lapalmaclub.it
Open 9pm–2am Mon–Thu, 9pm–3am Fri & Sat, sometimes
open Sun for special event

In recent years La Palma has become one of the very
best music venues in Rome. Consisting of two
impressive 18th-century country houses in a large
park, it provides a particularly wide range of culture
and entertainment. Among the many events laid on
are art exhibitions featuring such artists as Faccincani
and Berto, literary and theatrical events, live jazz gigs
with big-name musicians such as Dave Holland and
Paul Motian, and performances of classical music.
The weekends often feature club nights with sets by
cutting-edge DJs from home and abroad. Hungry
revellers can refuel at its good-value restaurant, Il
Bivacco, which serves modern Mediterranean cuisine,
including set menus of fresh fish, grilled meat or
pizza (call 06 4543 4457 for reservations).

Locanda Atlantide *medley of live music*
Via dei Lucani 22b • 06 4470 4540 • Tram lines Nos. 3 & 19 to Reti
>> www.locandatlantide.it Check website for opening times

Behind a deceptively plain metal door, Locanda
Atlantide is a dimly lit, spacious venue, housed in a
former warehouse. This alternative club arranges a
varied programme of cutting-edge DJ sets, live acts
and offbeat theatre. Expect garage, 60s sounds, punk
rock and jazz, sometimes by singer-songwriters.

Il Posto delle Fragole *Nordic treats* `9 H1`
Via Carlo Botta 51 • 06 4788 0959
>> www.ilpostodellefragole.org Open 8pm–2am Wed–Sun

The main room at this intimate Scandinavian-themed
cultural centre has a tiny stage for world-music
concerts and theatre performances. Scandinavian
food and drink, such as reindeer meat and gravadlax,
are available. Film screenings, chess nights and
Swedish-language courses are also on offer.

Casa del Jazz *jazz beats* `9 G5`
Viale di Porta Ardeatina 55 • 06 704731
>> www.casajazz.it Check website for opening times

The former headquarters of a criminal gang, Villa
Osio was confiscated by the State and turned into
this impressive venue by Rome's mayor and jazz buff
Walter Veltroni. Summer concerts in its park (with
seating for up to 1,000) are popular, as are Sunday
morning concerts featuring Dixieland jazz and brunch.

>> *Most live-music venues close or move to outdoor locations in the summer months*

Performance

Teatro dell'Opera di Roma *operatics* `5 F3`

Piazza Beniamino Gigli 1 • 06 4816 0255
»» www.opera.roma.it
Box office open 9am–5pm Tue–Sat, 9am–1:30pm Sun

Since opening in 1880, this opulent theatre has staged premieres such as Giacomo Puccini's *Tosca* and performances by singers such as Maria Callas. Today, you are more likely to see contemporary work than classic opera. The acoustics are faultless.

Spazio Boario–Villaggio Globale *tented global village* `8 C4`

Lungotevere Testaccio • 06 575 7233
»» www.ecn.org/villaggioglobale
Check website for opening times

Villaggio Globale is one of Rome's oldest *centri sociali* and boasts one of the city's most unusual locations – a 19th-century slaughterhouse. Before setting up the colourful Spazio Boario circus tent in the huge cattleyard in 2002, the Villaggio was sinking into decline. Now it's a popular venue with a great sound system, hosting frequent concerts by respected Italian and international artists – from ska heroes the Skatalites to reggae legend Tony Rebel. It is also home to Toretta Stile, an infrequent yet busy alternative night that journeys through the history of popular music. The admission fees are a bargain. Inside the main building, there is a stage for theatre and smaller performances. The tent is taken down in mid-May and concerts move outside until October.

For the very latest on Rome go to »» **www.realcity.dk.com**

Teatro Palladium *experimental venue* `10 C5`

Piazza Bartolomeo Romano 8 • 06 5706 7761
>> www.teatro-palladium.it Box office open 4–8pm
Wed–Mon, and to 9:30pm on performance days

This exciting space was once in danger of being
turned into a bingo hall. Instead, the 1920s theatre
was restored by Roma Trè university and it now stages
experimental art, electronic music, cutting-edge
theatre, political debate, literary lectures and film.

Classico Village *live music and theatre* `10 C5`

Via Giuseppe Libetta 3 • 06 574 3364
>> www.classico.it Open 8:30pm–1am Mon–Thu,
8:30pm–5am Fri & Sat

This warehouse-like club has two large rooms (both
with stages for concerts and DJs), a gorgeous outdoor
courtyard and a restaurant. It puts on an array of
events that cross all musical genres – Jeff Mills and
Suicide have both played here – as well as theatre.

Caffè Latino *a mix of music* `8 D4`

Via di Monte Testaccio 96 • 06 5728 8556
Opening times vary; call for details

Despite the name, this long-term resident of
Testaccio's clubbing district focuses on more than
just Latin-American sounds. It also serves up a
medley of funk, world music and jazz in a programme
of live concerts. The atmosphere is warm and inviting,
and the crowd lively and friendly.

Filmstudio *art-house cinema* `1 D5`

Via degli Orti d'Alibert 1c
06 6819 2987

Now returned to its former grandeur, this Trastevere
cinema is *the* place for film fanatics. Showings
include contemporary and historical independent
films and video-art that can't be seen anywhere else,
such as experimental shorts from the 1960s, some in
their original language *(versione originale)*.

Palacisalfa *large capacity venue*

Viale dell'Oceano Atlantico 271d • 06 5728 8018 • Ⓜ EUR Fermi
>> www.palacisalfa.com Check website for opening times

For years, Palacisalfa, in the EUR district, was Rome's
only location for mid-sized indoor concerts. Although
the acoustics are poor, this sports and live-music
venue has seen the likes of The Strokes and Placebo
play. Its prominence is fading, though, as the Auditorium, Palladium and Villaggio Globale gain ground.

Performance

Alexanderplatz *top-notch jazz* `1 B2`
Via Ostia 9 • 06 3974 2171
>> www.alexanderplatz.it Open 9pm–2am daily

Considered one of the best jazz clubs in Italy, Alexanderplatz hosts top Italian and international musicians, such as Enrico Pieranuzi and Lionel Hampton. In summer, it organizes the Villa Celimontana Festival *(see p134)*. Make a reservation, especially if you want dinner. Concerts start at 10:30pm.

Lettere Caffè *words and music* `8 C2`
Via San Francesco a Ripa 100–101 • 06 5833 4379
>> www.letterecaffe.org Open 4pm–2am daily

Lettere is a literary café that arranges poetry competitions, book presentations, readings, theatre evenings and plenty of live music, from jazz to folk and rock. Books and magazines are on sale in the front room. Food, tea and herbal infusions are served, as well as the usual alcoholic beverages.

Nuovo Sacher *independent films* `8 C2`
Largo Aschianghi 1
06 581 8116

Owned by leftist, award-winning Italian director Nanni Moretti, Nuovo Sacher often shows films ignored by mainstream distributors, some in their original language. Most summer screenings take place at the outdoor arena next to the cinema. This is one of the few Roman cinemas to have a bar and a bookshop.

Football Tickets and Traditions

Rivalry between AS Roma and SS Lazio runs so deep that new acquaintances often declare whether they are *romanisti* or *laziali*. For match tickets, go to merchandising shops **AS Roma Store** *(see p177)* and **Lazio Point** *(see p173)*, tobacconists with Lottomatica signs or to the Stadio Olimpico box office three hours before the match. Avid supporters, particularly season-ticket holders, sit in either of the *curve* (the ends of the stadium – south for Roma, north for Lazio). *Tribune* seats, on each side, are the best and most expensive. Snacks and drinks are available both inside and outside the stadium; join in a football tradition by ordering a *caffè Borghetti*, cold coffee with a dash of sambuca. No alcohol, cans or closed bottles are allowed inside.

Teatro India *industrial arts* `8 C5`
Via Luigi Pierantoni 6 • 06 6840 00346
>> www.teatrodiroma.net Tickets from Teatro Argentina box office 10am–2pm & 4–7pm Mon–Sat

Located in a fascinating and evocative 20th-century industrial zone next to the Tiber, this theatre has an international calendar of events, mixing classics with the avant garde. It has an experimental ethos and seeks to be a cultural meeting point between genres.

Big Mama *blues central* `8 C2`
Vicolo San Francesco a Ripa 18 • 06 581 2551
>> www.bigmama.it Check website for opening times

Big Mama is the place in Rome to listen to live blues, R&B, funk and soul. Well-known Italian and inter-national acts – such as Italian bluesman Roberto Ciotti and Jeff Healey – play the small stage, as do promising young local musicians. Concerts begin at 10:30pm; food and drink are on offer. Booking is advised.

Teatro Vascello *fresh dance and theatre* `8 A2`
Via Giacinto Carini 78 • 06 588 1021
>> www.teatrovascello.it Box office 3–8pm Tue–Sat, 3–6pm Sun

A stage for left-field theatre and contemporary dance, Teatro Vascello can be relied upon for keeping up with the latest cutting-edge companies. Innovative productions often rework traditional texts and mix video, digital arts and poetry with the work of young Italian playwrights.

Booking Tickets
Theatres and live-music venues do not always take telephone bookings. The best thing to do is either go to the box office or use a ticket agency. **Orbis** *(see p185)* sells tickets for sports events, theatres and most concerts, but charges a booking fee of about ten per cent. Many record stores sell tickets to rock, pop and jazz gigs; try or **Ricordi** *(see p185)*.

Teatro Ghione *big-name theatre* `1 C4`
Via delle Fornaci 37 • 06 637 2294
>> www.ghione.it Box office 10am–1pm & 4–8pm Tue–Sun

The Ghione's founders are husband-and-wife team Ileana Ghione, an Italian actress, and Christopher Axworthy, former professor at the Royal Academy of London. They renovated this former cinema to create one of Rome's most beautiful theatres, and now bring celebrated musicians and actors to the city.

bars & clubs

You'll be spoilt for choice when it comes to Rome's bar and club scene, which pulsates round the clock. Take your pick from an evening spent wine-tasting in an *enoteca*, sipping *mojitos* on a pool-side terrace or grooving to sounds spun by top international DJs. Or simply join the throng on one of the many café terraces, which are equipped with gas heaters and parasols for year-round action.

BARS AND CLUBS

In the last few years, the bar and club scene in this most ancient of cities has made significant strides towards modernity. Now that the *aperitivo* culture has seeped down from sophisticated Milan, there are increasingly attractive alternatives to the faux Irish pubs. Even the once grimy *centri sociali* are getting facelifts, drawing more stylish crowds and helping to put this most fashionable of capitals back on the map.

Jason Horowitz

Drinking Alfresco

The art of languishing at outdoor tables has been perfected at Trastevere, especially at **Bar San Calisto** *(see p119)*, though across the river, at the *centro storico*'s **Il Nolano** *(see p113)*, killing time is more of a fashion statement than a lifestyle. Another ideal spot to idle outdoors is the Art Nouveau **Caffè della Pace** *(see p113)*, just off Piazza Navona.

The Glitterati Set

The rather run-down Esquilino district has long been touted as the city's next big thing because of places like **Zest** *(see p116)*, the glamorous rooftop bar of the Radisson SAS ES.Hotel. The bars of the "golden triangle" *(see p120)* attract the beautiful people, in particular the **Bar del Fico** *(see p112)*, where both attire and surroundings are rather relaxed.

The T-word

Testaccio was once synonymous with tough, working-class Rome. These days, that image has been transformed thanks to a proliferation of nightspots. The café **Il Seme e La Foglia** *(see p118)* is a popular stopping off point for clubbers on their way to hip **Metaverso** *(see p118)* or **Akab** *(see p116)*, with its wide variety of music and other entertainment.

choice nightlife

Boogie Nights

It's common to see children eating ice cream on their fathers' shoulders after midnight, so it's no surprise that Romans grow up to be night owls. Brancaleone *(see p121)* has become more sophisticated, but still offers plenty of wild carousing, as does the House club **Goa** *(see p117)*. Testaccio, however, remains the centre of Rome's clubbing universe.

Laid-Back Locales

There is perhaps no city that exalts relaxation like Rome, and that is evident in the yuppie *aperitivo* bar **Friends Art Café** *(see p119)* and at **La Clandestina** *(see p115)*, which attracts a more alternative crowd. The crowds at **Stardust** *(see p120)* have thinned so it's more conducive to unwinding, while **Bohemien** *(see p115)* is a good laid-back gay bar.

Essential Enoteche

The city is full of watering holes, but why drink at some quasi-Irish pub when a charming wine bar is nearby? Try intimate **Enoteca Il Piccolo** *(see p113)* or the comfortable **Al Vino Al Vino** *(see p115)*, where regulars sip and chat. Or mix drinking with people-watching at **La Vineria** *(see p112)*, which means wine shop, but is really more of a singles bar.

La Vineria *sociable and lively* `6 C4`

Campo dei Fiori 15 • 06 6880 3268
Open 8:30am–2am Mon–Sat

One of Rome's open-air living rooms, this bar is the perfect place for a sociable apéritif. Cramped inside, with floor-to-ceiling wine racks, it's the outdoor tables that attract the masses, even in winter, when the smart crowd braves the elements to be seen here. Sooner or later, everyone will pass through La Vineria.

Crudo *a raw vibe* `7 E5`

Via degli Specchi 6 • 06 683 8989
≫ www.crudoroma.it Open 11:30am–2:30pm Mon, 11:30am–2:30pm & 6:30pm–2am Tue–Sat, 6:30pm–2am Sun

A bar, *enoteca* (wine bar) and restaurant each have a separate floor at this super-stylish venue. All the food served is raw, and there's also a choice of cocktails, wines and vegetable shakes – all reasonably priced. Just like the clientele, Crudo is dressed to impress.

Bar del Fico *coolest place under the sun* `6 C2`

Piazza del Fico 26–8 • 06 686 5205
Open 8:30am–2:30am Mon–Sat, noon–2:30am Sun

Spend some time at this destination bar and you'll discover why it has become such an institution. From the moment it opens right through to closing time, Del Fico is packed with a genial mix of locals and the cool crowd. On one table, you might find aspiring models comparing outfits, and on the next, a couple of old men passing the time over a game of chess. Whether you come early in the day for a coffee and a croissant, mid-evening for an apéritif and free nibbles, or late at night for a pre-club drinking session, you'll be in good company. The outdoor tables sit under the fig tree that lends its name to the bar and the small, cobblestoned square it's located on. Light lunches, including a buffet, a few hot dishes and *panini*, are served most days (noon–3pm Mon–Sat), and a varied brunch of international offerings (American-style or the more unusual Asian fare) is available on Sundays (noon–4pm).

Anima *dance for free* `6 D2`
Via Santa Maria dell'Anima 57 • 347 850 9256
Open 10:30pm–3am daily

This may be just the cheap night out you were looking for: where else in Rome can you get a steady mix of high-quality hip-hop, reggae and funk for free? The decor is designed to impress, but the upbeat vibe and friendly, lively crowd curb any pretension. Apéritifs are served in the early evening with a free buffet.

Caffè della Pace *legendary bar* `6 C2`
Via della Pace 3–7 • 06 686 1216
Open 9am–3am Tue–Sun, 4pm–3am Mon

A super-cool hang-out for the smart set, Della Pace has atmosphere in abundance. The resplendent Art Nouveau interior provides the perfect setting for journal-writing on a rainy day. And, when it's sunny, you can park yourself at a pavement table in front of the ivy-covered exterior and watch the world go by.

Enoteca il Piccolo *welcoming wine bar* `6 C3`
Via del Governo Vecchio 74–5 • 06 6880 1746
Open noon–3pm & 5pm–2am daily

Although just off Piazza Navona, this cosy *enoteca* is blissfully tourist-free. The first-class wine list (offered by the bottle and by the glass) draws the crowds in the early evening, when Romans meet for an after-work tipple. Try the home-made *fragolino* (strawberry liqueur) or the *sangria con frutti di bosco* (with forest berries).

Il Nolano *absorbingly romantic* `6 D4`
Campo dei Fiori 11–12 • 06 687 9344
Open 6pm–1:45am Mon–Fri, noon–1:45am Sat & Sun

The tables and old, wooden cinema chairs in the piazza outside this wine bar are often packed. Inside, however, it's quiet, intimate and full of character: the paint is peeling off the walls, there's a mishmash of furniture, and it's softly lit by fairy lights and table-top candles. This is a place for wooing.

Bars & Clubs

La Maison   *a key venue*   `6 D3`
Vicolo dei Granari 4 • 06 683 3312
Open Sep–May: 11:30pm–5am Tue–Sun (Jun–Aug: call 349 297 0731 for times)

A chic, chandelier-lit club for well-off thirty- and forty-something fashionistas, La Maison tries hard to maintain an exclusive reputation. Still, the door staff are ultra-helpful, the crowd friendly and the music less commercial than in many Roman clubs.

Supperclub   *palatial club*   `7 E3`
Via dei Nari 14 • 06 6830 1011
>> www.supperclub.com
Open 6:30pm–2am daily

A night at Supperclub is a multisensory experience that will raise your clubbing expectations forever. This elite venue, in a 16th-century palace, is a lounge, restaurant and club all in one. The younger twin of the same-name venue in Amsterdam, it shares a similar philosophy: to give you the best night out of your life. Start off with a long, cool drink in the long, cool lounge-bar. Then move on to one of the massive bed-sized sofas for a four-course dinner (from 9:15pm, 60€ excluding drinks, reservations essential). The menu combines local and international dishes and changes every couple of days. During dinner you can watch performance art; later you might like to indulge in a free massage from an in-house masseur. Then head downstairs for a dance. The lounge and club are open to non-diners, but entry is at the doorman's discretion.

Antica Enoteca di Via della Croce   *venerable wine bar*   `4 C2`
Via della Croce 76b • 06 679 0896
Open 11am–1am daily

This *enoteca* is a local institution, and has been going since about 1840. It's popular for apéritifs and wines by the glass. The wine list is wide-ranging and changes regularly, so check the blackboard. Unlike most bars, this place charges for the *aperitivo* buffet.

Antico Caffè Greco *from a bygone era* `4 D2`
Via Condotti 86 • 06 679 1700
Open 9am–7:30pm Tue–Sat, 10:30am–7pm Sun & Mon

Founded in 1760, the genteel Greco once attracted an artistic clientele ranging from German composer Richard Wagner to literary figures such as Goethe, Lord Byron and Mark Twain. Today, its history and comfortable sofas draws plenty of tourists – so stick with the locals, who prefer to stand at the bar.

Bohemien *casual gay bar* `5 F5`
Via degli Zingari 36 • 328 173 0158
Open 10am–2pm & 5pm–2am Tue–Sun

The stylish decor at Bohemien attracts a surprisingly unpretentious crowd. Under the soft light cast by an imposing 18th-century crystal chandelier, friendly actors, designers and wannabes sip on French, Portuguese and Spanish wines while perusing the art, photography and design books that are on sale.

Al Vino al Vino *fantastic wine list* `5 E5`
Via dei Serpenti 19 • 06 485 803
Open 5:30pm–12:30am Sun–Thu, 5:30pm–1:30am Fri & Sat

The international crowd at this light and airy *enoteca* chooses from affordable wines sourced by cordial owner Luca Camero, including the broadest selection of *passiti* (sweet wines) in town. The menu includes Sicilian specialities, such as *caponata* (sweet and sour aubergine stew) and *torte rustiche* (savoury cakes).

La Clandestina *laid-back style*
Via dei Volsci 33 • 06 444 0467 • Tram Nos. 3 & 19 to Reti
Open 8pm–3am daily

Sited opposite "32", one of Rome's oldest and best-known *centri sociali (see p99)*, this late-night wine bar pulls a trendy crowd that wanders between both places, catching up with old friends and making new ones. This is one of the few worthwhile bars in San Lorenzo, which is otherwise packed with Irish pubs.

Zest *out of this world* `5 H4`
Radisson SAS ES.Hotel, Via Filippo Turati 171 • 06 444 84762
>> www.rome.radissonsas.com Open 10am–1:30am daily

An unusual view over Rome's bustling but run-down Esquilino district and incredibly sleek interiors make Zest not only a great bar but also an unusual find in a city where classy minimalist design is rare. Located on the top floor of the Radisson SAS Hotel, Zest sits alongside Sette restaurant *(see p38)*, the hotel's swimming pool and the spa. The interior opens out on to the contemporary pool-side terrace, which is beautifully lit at night. Sitting outside languidly sipping an *aperitivo* is pure heaven.

There's a limited choice of wine by the glass, but the range of cocktails, mixed by beautiful, black-clad staff, is excellent. Snacks (sandwiches, salads and olives) are served and there is a small selection of main meals (including at least one meat, one fish and one pasta option each day). Service is sophisticated and refined, as is the clientele.

Coming Out *bustling gay hang-out* `9 G1`
Via San Giovanni in Laterano 8 • 06 700 9871
>> www.comingout.it Open 5pm–5am daily

This lively, unpretentious gay bar is always packed and is open from late afternoon until the early hours. Pre- and post-club rendezvous take place to a pop and revival soundtrack. In summer, the crowd spills out on to the pavement, from where there's a stunning view of the Colosseum.

Akab *a moveable feast* `8 D4`
Via di Monte Testaccio 69 • 06 572 50585
Open 11pm–4am Tue–Sun

Akab's varied programme, from house to R&B, has kept it in favour for years. It gets especially busy at the weekend and on Tuesdays for the electronic night, so expect queues. Both the lively street-level area and the more mellow basement host DJs and occasional live acts, and there's a short-film festival here every winter.

Caruso Caffè de Oriente *salsa sounds* `8 C4`
Via di Monte Testaccio 36 • 06 574 5019
Open 10:30pm–3am Tue–Thu & Sun, 11pm–4am Fri & Sat

There's a warm buzz to Oriente, with its orange-tinged walls and breezy summer terrace. Although primarily focused on Latin and R&B, with lots of salsa, this club has also been known to slip into commercial disco from time to time. It features live acts, predominantly playing Latino music, almost every night.

Ex Magazzini *established club* `10 B3`
Via dei Magazzini Generali 8b • 06 575 8040
Open 10pm–2am Tue–Thu & Sun, 10pm–5am Fri & Sat

Ex Magazzini's music policy avoids the mainstream; the club plays host to Rome's best alternative DJs and attracts a fringe crowd. The venue is on two levels, with a glass panel set in the ground floor for checking out what's happening in the cavern-like basement. On Sunday afternoons, it opens for a small flea market.

Distillerie Clandestine *eat, drink, club* `10 C5`
Via Libetta 13 • 06 5730 5102
>> www.distillerieclandestine.com Open 8:30pm–4:45am Tue–Sat

This spacious bar-restaurant-disco was one of the first to meet the demand for multipurpose venues, and it's still one of the best. Two of the three rooms are for eating and drinking, the other for dancing. The soundtrack to the night combines DJ sets with live music – such as live sax played over nu-jazz, lounge or funk. Spacious and buzzing from mid-evening until the early hours, Clandestine is ultra cool.

Gay Club Nights
Rome's gay scene is small but sparkling. Most gay nights at clubs cater for both men and women, as there are few exclusively for lesbians. Good weekly nights are Friday's popular Mucca Assassina (literally Murderous Cow) at **Qube** *(see p174)* and Omogenic at **Circolo degli Artisti** *(see p119)*; on Saturdays, head for Queer at **Piper** *(see p172)* or

Gorgeous at **Classico Village** *(see p105)*. One Thursday a month, **Locanda Atlantide** *(see p103)* hosts Coq Madame, and one Sunday a month, **Goa** *(see p118)* is home to the lesbian Venus Rising. In summer, most nights move to the open-air Gay Village festival (www.gayvillage.it) in Testaccio. Club nights are always opening and closing, so keep up to date by checking www.gayroma.it.

Bars & Clubs

Goa *international bright young things*
10 C5

Via Libetta 13 • 06 574 8277

Open 11pm–4am Tue–Sun (closed end May to end Sep)

Rome's best house and dance club is hard to get into and the drinks are pricey, but the fact that it hosts respected Italian and international DJs – from Italy's own superstar-DJ Claudio Coccoluto to Howie B – makes it the hippest of the hip. Goa also co-hosts week-night concerts with Brancaleone *(see p121)*.

Metaverso *experimental music and space*
8 C4

Via di Monte Testaccio 38a • 06 574 4712

>> www.metaverso.com   Open 7pm–4am Tue–Sat

Tucked away among the predominantly unremarkable discos of Testaccio, this venue nevertheless stands out. It hosts Rome's best alternative DJs, plus a few stars from respected global labels such as Metalheadz. Its tiny, vaulted rooms fill up in the early hours with a trendy media and arts crowd. It also holds gay nights.

Alpheus *four for one*
8 D5

Via del Commercio 36 • 06 574 7826

>> www.alpheus.it   Open 10pm–4am (phone to check)

The vast space of the Alpheus is divided into four distinct areas, so on some nights you can choose between theatre, cabaret, a live gig or a Latin American, hip-hop or house-fuelled disco. Occasionally all rooms are given over to popular one-nighters, such as the Kinder Gaärden (mainly) gay bash.

Jungle Club *dark tendencies*
8 D4

Via di Monte Testaccio 95 • 333 720 8694

>> www.jungleclubroma.com   Open 10:45pm–4:30am Fri & Sat

Appearing to be just another closed-door venue, Jungle Club rises from the grave each weekend with its famous Saturday goth nights. Black-clad fans adorned with studded collars and pallid complexions gather here to listen to the heavy hits of yesteryear. A must for die-hard Cure fans.

Il Seme e La Foglia *an easy-going vibe*
8 D4

Via Galvani 18 • 06 574 3008

Open 8am–2am Mon–Sat, 6pm–1:30am Sun

Set right in the middle of Testaccio, the clubbing district, Il Seme e la Foglia is one of Rome's more fashionable fixtures. The convivial café is both a local haunt where friends come to chat over a quick lunch (mostly salads and *panini*) and a meeting point for clubbers wanting a pre-dance drink.

Circolo degli Artisti *boogie nights* `10 D2`
Via Casilina Vecchia 42 • 06 7030 5684
>> www.circoloartisti.it Check website for opening times

Circolo, as it's known locally, features disco nights, including popular gay evenings, and plenty of live bands playing a range of musical genres, from easy listening to punk rock. Inside, the acoustics can be poor, but in summer the leafy garden is a perfect spot for dancing under the stars.

Bar San Calisto *pure and simple* `8 C1`
Piazza San Calisto 3–4 • 06 583 5869
Open 6am–1:30am Mon–Sat

This is one of the last in a vanishing breed of old-style Roman bars that offer a no-frills service in neon-lit surroundings. A nice change from the touristy bars around the corner on Piazza Santa Maria in Trastevere, it's packed day and night with an interesting crowd of aspiring artists, left-wing activists and old-timers.

Friends Art Café *pre-dinner drinking* `8 C1`
Piazza Trilussa 34 • 06 581 6111
Open 7:30am–2am Mon–Sat, 6:30pm–2am Sun

Lively and crowded at almost every hour of the day and night, this slick Plexiglas-and-chrome bar is best enjoyed at *aperitivo* time, when there's a generous free buffet. A few trips to replenish your plate with pasta and rice salads, mini-omelettes and small *panini* can easily turn nibbling into a light dinner.

Whet the Appetite

Aperitivo is sacred in Rome; dinner's prelude stimulates both taste buds and conversation. Most bars offer free snacks at apéritif time. For great views, and a treat, head to either the **Hotel Eden** terrace *(see p142)* or the roof bar of the **Raphael Hotel** *(see p170)*. The latter is lovely in summer, as is **Ciampini al Cafè du Jardin** *(see p172)*, at the top of the Spanish Steps.

Early evening see piazzas fill with drinkers at outdoor tables; try **Ciampini** *(see p170)* in Piazza San Lorenzo in Lucina or any of the bars in Campo dei Fiori. Across the river, in Trastevere, stop at **Enoteca Ferrara** *(see p36)*, with its great choice of wines, or at **Friends Art Café** *(see above)*. Out east are **Trimani Enoteca** *(see p68)*, chic **Zest** *(see p116)* and **Bar Marani** *(see p174)*, which is great for chips and Campari Soda.

Bars & Clubs

In Vino Veritas Art Bar *cosy corner* `8 B1`
Via Garibaldi 2a • 339 446 3371
Open 3pm–2am Tue–Sun

The In Vino Veritas Art Bar is a much more relaxing venue than its name might suggest. Yes, there is art on the walls – and it puts on the occasional theatrical or musical performance – but this is also one of the places in Trastevere to sit back and perhaps enjoy tea in the afternoon and a cocktail or two in the evening.

Stardust *late-night lovelies* `8 C1`
Vicolo dei Renzi 4 • 06 5832 0875
Open 4pm–2am Mon–Sat, noon–2am Sun

This intimate Trastevere bar is a meeting point for a mix of international night owls; expect conversations with strangers to go on long into the night, way past the official closing time. Crêpes, quiches and *panini* are available every evening, and there's an American-style brunch on Sunday afternoons.

Irish and British Pubs
Most of Rome's Irish- and British-themed pubs are home from home for foreign students; few have any real character. Among the best are **Trinity College** *(see p170)*, a *centro storico* fixture with an international crowd; **The Fiddler's Elbow** *(see p174)* in Monti; and Trastevere's **Molly Malone** *(see p177)*, favoured by Anglophile locals.

Ombre Rosse *relaxing drinks* `8 B1`
Piazza Sant'Egidio 12 • 06 588 4155
Open 8am–2am Mon–Sat, 6pm–2am Sun

This is one of Trastevere's most fashionable bars, with tables on the pretty piazza all year round and a staunch local following. Ombre Rosse offers a wide range of national and imported beers, wines and cocktails, and a good selection of salads and snacks. There is also live jazz on Fridays.

Pre-club Hanging Out
Nights out start late in Rome, so early evening socializing tends to be a laid-back affair in one of the city's numerous pre-club hang outs. The venue *par excellence* is the *centro storico*'s Campo dei Fiori, with its scores of bars and buzzing (and at times rowdy) atmosphere. In the "golden triangle" (around Piazza del Fico) the crowds have lots of flash to match their cash, while over in Trastevere, **Bar San Caliso** *(see p119)* is poplular with a more alternative and creative crowd. Students and the left-wing crowd, however, tend to hang out in the early evening at **Bar Marani** *(see p119)*. Outside the city centre, the humble kiosk on the Ponte Milvio pedestrian bridge is another place popular with Rome's well-to-do party animals.

Brancaleone *squatting heaven*

Via Levanna 11, Montesacro • 06 8200 4382
Train to Nomentana
>> www.brancaleone.it Open 10pm–4am Thu–Sat (for music), 8pm–1:30am Tue & Sun (for cinema); see website for events

Rome's king of clubs, this super-professional *centro sociale (see p99)* hosts the very best Italian and international DJs. It often features the likes of Goldie, Talvin Singh and Kruder & Dorfmeister, offering a mix of underground and mainstream music at prices that won't break the bank. Fridays at Brancaleone with the Agatha crew have entered the history annals of Roman electronic music, while Saturdays are geared towards house. The interior, a mix of steel sculptures and sleek design, is improved most years by the squat's organizers. The squat's members are politically active in the northern suburbs, where the club is located, and they carry out work in the local community. They also run an in-house organic-products shop. Upstairs, there is a cinema and an organic café, which also hosts art exhibitions.

streetlife

If the sun is shining, be it summer or winter, Romans leave their houses to hang out *all'aperto* (in the open). From festivals among ancient ruins to daily food markets in piazzas, life is lived out on the street. Beyond the historic centre, many neighbourhoods still retain their individual characters, though a combination of gentrification and global influence is bringing inevitable waves of change.

Ghetto *Jewish district* 7 F5

This once-walled-off enclave is today a distinct and lively area, its tiny streets dotted with bakeries, textile shops and artisans' workshops. Life here follows the rhythms of the Jewish week, so businesses are shut on Saturday and open on Sunday. The Via del Portico d'Ottavia is the focal point of the Ghetto, filling up on Friday evenings and Sunday mornings with teenagers on mopeds, families with pushchairs and old men chatting. At the bottom of the street is the huge synagogue, housing the Museo d'Arte Ebraica *(see p183)*, which explores the long history of Jewish people in Rome. Further up is cross-street Via della Reginella, lined with shops selling antiquarian and second-hand books, which leads up to the Fontana delle Tartarughe *(see p86)*. Refuel on chunky blocks of cake dough stuffed with dried fruits and spices or the sublime chocolate-and-ricotta tarts at Pasticceria Ebraica "Il Buccione" *(see p58)*, or grab a slice of delicious kosher pizza from Zi Fenizia *(see p179)*.

Around Piazza del Fico *lively hub* 6 C2

Deceptively quiet by day, these cobbled lanes are central Rome's hippest enclave and limousine park by night. The young and the beautiful flock here, with the old and rich hot on their heels. There's a swell around *aperitivo* time, but the real action doesn't start until close to midnight, when outdoor tables are fiercely contested at the area's two key bars, Caffè della Pace *(see p113)* and Bar del Fico *(see p112)*.

Flea Markets

Porta Portese (Sun only; *see p181*), the mother of Roman flea markets, is sprawling and eclectic. Russian binoculars, bicycle parts, Venetian chandeliers and oriental rugs are among the wares on sale at stalls that extend from the Porta Portese bridge to Trastevere station. Cheap modern clothes predominate, but there are still some great finds on the second-hand stalls at the Porta Portese end. For antiques and bric-a-brac, focus on Via Ippolito Nievo. Come at 7:30am for the best buys and be prepared to elbow your way through the crowds. Bargain hard and beware of pickpockets. Some dedicated bargain-hunters prefer the more manageable **Via Sannio** (*see p181*) covered market for clothes (Mon–Sat). Prices drop at the end of the week.

Piazza San Lorenzo in Lucina `4 C3`

This traffic-free piazza with its chilled-out bars and cafés doubles as a living room for the affluent residents of Rome's historic centre. Furs, small dogs, immaculate suits and designer sunglasses are *de rigueur*. A morning coffee or a midday apéritif at historic bar Ciampini *(see p170)* is worth the steep prices for the schmooze factor. And the square's church of San Lorenzo in Lucina *(see p182)* even houses Bernini busts.

Piazza Navona *central hang-out* `6 D2`

Surrounded by stunning pastel-coloured palazzos, this piazza is an ideal place to sit back and watch the world go by. Order a *gelato*, a coffee or a glass of *prosecco* at one of the cafés and take in the scene: street performers, from human statues to mandolin-players and jongleurs, make regular appearances, while artists sell work – from uninspiring watercolours to surprisingly good portraits – at the centre of the piazza.

Campo dei Fiori *by day and night* `6 D4`

The picturesque Campo dei Fiori has a split personality – pretty and down-to-earth by day, lively and fun-filled by night. In the morning, a fairly average fruit-and-vegetable market dominates. Stallholders will tell you that their family has been there for five generations or more, but prices aren't what they used to be. Recently, the market has acquired a small organic stall selling vegetables, plants, herbs and seeds. Nearby, cobblestoned streets hide boutiques and designer shoe stores. Towards evening, the Campo becomes a meeting point, as the bars and cafés spill out on to the square. Long-term residents prefer the historic La Vineria *(see p112)* for an *aperitivo* (a glass of *prosecco* here is just 1.50€), though the other bars around the piazza are equally good for some unabashed people-watching. Groups of youngsters gravitate to the statue of Giordano Bruno, burned at the stake here in 1600 for being a little too freethinking for the Catholic Church.

Streetlife

Piazzale di Ponte Milvio *lively piazza*

On the border of Rome's wealthy northern suburbs, this piazza is the haunt of Rome's young and loaded. On summer evenings, it heaves with rich kids on scooters and in Smart cars. The centre of the action is the tiny kiosk on the piazza that sells *grattachecche* (grated ice-and-syrup drinks). Lovebirds tend to slip off for a romantic moment on the massive Ponte Milvio, one of Rome's few pedestrian-only bridges.

Parco della Musica *cultural hot spot*   `2 C2`

Viale Pietro de Coubertin 30
BArt: 06 8024 1437; ReD: 06 8069 1630
\gg www.auditoriumroma.com

From temporary art exhibitions to fine food, world-class concerts to picnics in the outdoor amphitheatre, the arts-and-leisure complex of Parco della Musica has attractions aplenty. Guided tours of the scarab-shaped concert halls *(see p102)* provide a lesson in acoustics and the background of the centre.

When hunger strikes, head to either the airy BArt for sandwiches and snacks, or ReD (short for *ristorante e design; see p179*) for contemporary Roman cuisine. It's not just the food that's on sale here – you can also buy the chair you're sitting on or the paintings on the wall (all listed on a separate menu). What's more, it's open late for post-concert dining. The on-site bookshop and music store have excellent classical sections, including rare recordings and manuscripts. In winter, an ice-skating rink is often set up in the amphitheatre.

Via Veneto *style from a bygone era*   `5 E2`

First made famous by Federico Fellini's 1960 film *La Dolce Vita*, this street has come alive again. Ironically, this has only happened since the efforts by local businesses to cash in on the "sweet life" have stopped. Chic boutiques and luxury hotels line the top half of the street. Lower down, the vibe gets funkier, with the Lamborghini showroom housing contemporary art, accessories and, of course, cars.

Villa Borghese *cultural park*

>> www.villaborghese.it
Park open dawn–sunset daily

Romans use this vast urban green space to unwind, show off, cool down and hang out. Bicycles (from bike-hire stands around the park) or pedal-rickshaws (for hire in Viale dei Bambini) are the ideal way to explore the formal gardens, statues and fountains, though many young Romans prefer to skate. Boats are also for hire on the artificial lake.

Enhancing its cultural quota, Villa Borghese has recently acquired a perfect replica of Shakespeare's Globe Theatre (Teatro Silvano Toti Globe). Additionally, the park is home to the Galleria Borghese *(see p84)*,

the Museo Nazionale di Villa Giulia *(see p183)* – which exhibits Etruscan artifacts – and the Galleria Nazionale d'Arte Moderna *(see p85)*, which has a sunny outdoor café. Cultural and sporting events from international showjumping (May–Jun) to t'ai chi demonstrations, ballet performances and concerts on the Pincio terrace *(see p132)* take place regularly.

There's another café, with shady outdoor tables, in Viale dei Bambini, but the park's party heart is definitely the Piazza di Siena Art Caffè *(see p172)*. In summer (Jun–Aug), it's a popular outdoor haunt, with art installations, live music and fashion shows until 4am. In winter, the bar moves underground to the Villa Borghese car park, for more of the same.

Streetlife

San Lorenzo *political hotbed*
Nowhere else in the world are you likely to see bomb-damaged buildings from WWII, a "hemporium" (dope shop), a Chapel of Miracles and Che Guevara murals all on the same block. Once an anarchist stronghold, the San Lorenzo area, southeast of Termini, is now a haunt of artists, intellectuals and students. Via dei Volsci and Via degli Acqui are full of tiny bars, cheap pizzerias and artists' studios.

Monti *ancient and modern* `5 E4`
The notorious Suburra slum of ancient Rome, birthplace of Julius Caesar, is now the centrepoint of Monti, a once rough-and-ready area that is just about staving off gentrification and maintaining a delicate balance between the old and the new. Artisans' workshops (jewellery-makers, picture framers, art restorers) dot this neighbourhood of comprises steep cobbled streets lined with ivy-covered apartments.

Piazza Vittorio District *melting pot* `5 G5`
Rome's bustling international quarter radiates out from this piazza's leafy public gardens and arcaded buildings. The chaotic fruit-and-vegetable market that once surrounded the square has now moved to a nearby indoor location on Via Principe Amedeo. Halal butchers, spice-sellers straight from Asia, and African women selling beans make this Rome's most ethnically diverse area. The Chinese presence is evident in the clothes and trinket stores, as well as the early-morning t'ai chi classes in the piazza.

The gardens in the centre of the square contain the ruins of the Porta Magica, with its curious alchemic inscriptions, and just to the west is MAS *(see p180)*, a huge emporium with everything from French navy-issue jackets to Moroccan slippers. At the other end of the piazza is Il Palazzo del Freddo di Giovanni Fassi *(see p30)*, a *gelateria* that serves *caterinetta*, an ice-cream log. For a nearby coffee stop, try the dramatic bar at the Teatro Ambra Jovinelli *(see p102)*.

For the very latest on Rome go to >> www.realcity.dk.com

Testaccio Food Market *local produce* `8 D3`

More than just a market, this is a community centre-point for a working-class neighbourhood that has, so far, resisted gentrification. Things start humming at around 7:30am, as working folk stop by for essentials. Towards noon, indomitable grannies come for supplies; follow them to find the best seasonal produce. The day after a football match, you'll have to dodge the verbal crossfire between stallholders – this is AS Roma heartland. The theatrical sporting debate continues in the Bar Zi Elena *(see p175)* across the road.

Produce straight from the farm has dwindled, but you can still catch a whiff of *rucola selvatica* (wild rocket) among the few remaining vegetable stands in this covered market. Offal is popular here, although hygiene laws mean you'll no longer see lamb's stomach on display. Rows of *alimentari* offer bulging *caciotta* cheeses, cod fillets and *prosciutto*; get a *panino* made up and picnic in the local gardens, but get here before 2pm, when the market starts to pack up.

Garbatella *experimental housing project* `10 C5`

The area of Garbatella was created in the 1920s to house blue-collar workers and their families, whose homes had been destroyed by Mussolini's building of a highway from Palazzo Venezia to the Colosseum. There's a strong sense of community here today, though the old working-class inhabitants are now mixed with students and arty, middle-class types. Best visited by foot or on a scooter, much of the unique architecture, modelled on the English garden cities, is still intact. Great importance was given to outdoor spaces – the huge courtyards are used as playgrounds.

Start at Piazza Bartolomeo Romano and explore *lotto* (plot) 8. Stroll up to Piazza Brin and lunch at the Trattoria Moschino *(see p179)*, overlooking the old gasworks. Next door is *lotto* 5, where each apartment has its own *orto* (vegetable garden). There are two "hotels" – Albergo Rosso and Albergo Bianco – which provide communal living for evicted families. The May *festa* here brings up-and-coming bands to every piazza.

havens

Turn down a side road off any busy street and you'll discover a cobbled alley or hidden piazza in which to take refuge. The city's many public parks offer similar solace and epitomize Rome's charm – elegant, slightly scruffy and quite simply beautiful. Taking into account the luxurious spas, leafy gardens, open-air pools and quiet café terraces that are also available, peace and quiet is easy to find in Rome.

Water-Bus on the Tiber *cruising along* `6 B1`
Depart from Ponte Sant'Angelo • 06 678 9361
» www.battellidiroma.it Book for all tours

For a calmer view of Rome, take to the river. Boats leave from Ponte Sant'Angelo at 10am, 11:30am, 3:30pm and 5pm. The round trip via Isola Tiberina *(see p80)* takes 70 minutes (10€). There's also a return trip to Ostia Antica *(see p95)* from Ponte Marconi (metro Basilica San Paolo) at 9:15am (11€).

Rialto Sant'Ambrogio *halcyon squat* `7 F5`
Via Sant'Ambrogio 4 • 06 6813 3640
» www.rialtosantambrogio.org Check website for times

Dedicated to the promotion of jazz, experimental music, theatre, cinema, art and photography – with regular festivals and exhibitions – this old palazzo is now a quiet and peaceful *centro sociale (see p99)*. The candle-lit courtyard is a wonderful summer-evening refuge from the bustle of the Ghetto outside.

Rome's Parks

Rome has no shortage of public parks, most of which were once the gardens of grand villas and palaces or the hunting grounds of princes, popes and kings. The most popular in central Rome is **Villa Borghese** *(see p127)*; its extensive leafy grounds contain world-famous museums – including the Galleria Borghese *(see p84)* and the Galleria Nazionale d'Arte Moderna *(see p85)* – as well as all manner of buildings of architectural interest, a lake, a riding school and a zoo. In summer, it's the venue for many theatre and music shows, as well as the base for bikers, skaters and strollers. From here you can take the footbridge to the **Pincio** *(see p172)* gardens to soak up the picture-postcard view of St Peter's dome in the background and Piazza del Popolo just below.

The largest public park in central Rome is **Villa Pamphili** *(see p177)*, which lies between the Vatican and Monteverde. It's a popular spot for jogging and family trips – children love feeding the turtles in the pond and riding the ponies. Close by is the **Parco del Gianicolo** *(see p177)*, from where there are splendid views across the city. Down towards Trastevere is the enchanting, if rather small, **Villa Sciarra** *(see p177)*, with its luxurious landscaped garden. If you are in Rome between April and June, or in October, have a look at the **Roseto Comunale** (municipal rose garden; *see p176)*, as this is when the flowers are in bloom. **Villa Torlonia** *(see p174)*, not far from Termini, is a great spot for a stroll or a picnic; the gardens contain two ornate fountains, one of which was designed by Bernini. Further northwest, the huge **Villa Ada** *(see p172)*, the former hunting grounds of the Savoy royal family, is arguably Rome's most beautiful park. Under its ancient holm oak trees, you can almost forget you are in a metropolis, so wild is it in parts.

Hotel de Russie *pampering treat* `4 C1`
Via del Babuino 9 • 06 328 881
>> www.hotelderussie.it
Spa and gym 7am–9pm daily; treatments 9am–9pm daily

It may look stylish and exclusive, but the spa at this grand hotel is open to all. If a day in the Turkish bath, sauna and gym (35€) is not enough, add on a treatment or two: massages and body treatments, including shiatsu, cost from 90€; facials from 50€.

Aveda Spa *the beauty of nature* `4 D2`
Rampa Mignanelli 9 • 06 6992 4886
>> www.avedaroma.com
Open 3:30–8pm Mon, 10:30am–7:30pm Tue–Sat

Aveda may be a brand, but this city spa is far from impersonal. After being greeted with a cup of herbal tea, you'll be shown to one of the calming treatment rooms. Try a hydrotherm massage (85€), a purifying and hydrating facial (80€) or some mud therapy (77€).

Piscina dell'Hotel Parco dei Principi *swimming in luxury* `3 F5`
Via Frescobaldi 5 • 06 854 421
>> www.parcodeiprincipi.com Open May–Sep 10am–7pm daily

This large open-air pool, set in the leafy gardens of an elegant hotel, is the best place in central Rome for a swim. It's rarely crowded, due in no small part to the rather pricey entrance charge from 35€ (45€ weekends). Lunch is available at the poolside café-bar.

Caffè Capitolino *coffee with a view* `7 G5`
Piazzale Caffarelli • 06 6919 0564
>> www.museicapitolini.org Open 9am–8pm Tue–Sun

It's not very well known, but the terrace at this low-key café in the Musei Capitolini has a spectacular view over the domes and rooftops of Rome. Whether it's for breakfast, lunch or an *aperitivo*, you can relax under the shade of a large parasol. Enter from the museum or from the separate entrance on the piazza.

>> *Take a boat up the Tiber for a romantic dinner (43€; booking essential on 06 678 9361)*

Havens

Villa Celimontana *perfect for a stroll* `9 G2`

Once the garden of the Mattei family villa, this well-kept park contains ancient ruins from the family collection, including an Egyptian obelisk. A short walk from the Colosseum and the Forum, it's a perfect place for some post-sightseeing recuperation. The swings and fishpond are popular attractions. On summer evenings, the candle-lit park hosts big-name musicians for the Jazz & Image Festival *(see p17)*.

Giardino degli Aranci *peace and quiet* `8 D2`

A little walled garden dotted with orange trees and slightly overgrown, Aranci (also known as Parco Savello) boasts one of the most stunning views of Rome. If you come for the sunset, you'll have to pick your way through hand-holding couples; it's a popular romantic spot. At other times, particularly in the early morning, you will always be able find a peaceful spot all to yourself.

Cimitero Acattolico *garden of rest* `8 D4`
Via Caio Cestio 6 • 06 574 1900
>> www.protestantcemetery.it
Open 9am–4:30pm Mon–Sat

The so-called "Protestant cemetery" – which is actually filled with the graves and tombs of all kinds of non-Catholics – is completely bewitching. After John Keats was laid to rest here in 1821, his friend and fellow poet Percy Bysshe Shelley, whose ashes are also interred here, was inspired to state "It might make one in love with death to know that one should be buried in so sweet a place." Their neighbours below ground include Antonio Gramsci, Italy's seminal anti-fascist thinker, and August Goethe, son of German writer and philosopher J W Goethe. Stroll among the cypresses and tropical palms looking at some of the statuary; the tombs of American sculptors and painters Franklyn Simmons and William Story are both amazing. Admission is free, but consider leaving some coins in the donation box to help with the upkeep.

Parco Regionale dell'Appia Antica
Visitors' centre: Via Appia Antica 58–60 • Bus Nos. 118, 218
>> www.parcoappiaantica.org • 06 512 6314

This vast park may abut the city wall, but it is pure open country – you wouldn't think you were near a capital city. Extending 16 km (10 miles) south and east, its spine is the Appia Antica, Rome's first Imperial highway, built in 312 BC. Enter the park through the ancient San Sebastiano gate and you'll see a scene of moss-covered ruins dotted across fields and hills.

Romans walk or cycle the Appia on Sundays, when it's partly pedestrianized, but there are plenty of places to explore off-route any day. Check out the "Domine Quo Vadis?" church (where Peter is said to have seen the risen Christ) or the Roman racetrack complete with grandstands. Free guided tours on foot and by bike depart from the visitors' centre (which also hires out bikes), and there's a hop-on hop-off Archaeobus *(see website for details)*. If you want a stop-off, there are eight restaurants along the Appia.

Bar-Ristorante Zodiaco *lovers' terrace*
Viale del Parco Mellini 88–90 • 06 3549 6744 • Ⓜ Ottaviano
>> www.zodiacoroma.it
Open 10am–1am Mon–Thu & Sun, 10am–3am Fri & Sat

The large terrace at this bar and restaurant high on the verdant Monte Mario hill commands a stunning view over the city. Romans bring their true loves to this romantic spot to watch the sunset with a cocktail or two. It's equally impressive at any time of day.

Orto Botanico *wild life* 8 B1
Largo Cristina di Svezia 24 • 06 686 4193   Open summer 9:30am–7pm Tue–Sat; winter 9am–4pm Mon–Sat

Rome's botanic garden, with its shady alleys, ancient trees and Baroque fountains, is slightly dishevelled, but that only adds to its charm. Over 7,000 plant species are grown here, including a fine spread of orchids. Don't miss the amazing view of Rome from the bench at the top of the park. **Adm**

hotels

Charming little B&Bs, boutique hotels and luxurious residences are all part of the new and improved Roman hotel market. Most hoteliers renovated and upgraded before the Jubilee in 2000, so even the cheaper places tend to have updated decor, air conditioning, satellite TV and modem connections. As a result, however, prices have risen significantly and a bargain bed is now hard to find.

HOTELS

Beatification ceremonies, school trips and trade fairs can easily swallow up hotel space, so if you're fussy about where you stay, book well ahead. Cheap hotels are hard to find, but B&Bs now plug the gap and offer a personal touch. Boutique and designer hotels add extra choice in the mid-range. I recommend weighing up the advantages of location over price; being able to stroll out of the door onto a cobbled lane in the city centre is worth the extra euros.

Frances Kennedy

Designer Dreams

Immerse yourself in Italian design by staying at **Radisson SAS ES.Hotel** *(see p146)*, a blissful marriage of slick minimalism and state-of-the-art creature comforts. **Hotel Art** *(see p141)* offers an audacious interior decor, while **Hotel Aleph** *(see p143)* has theatrical, over-the-top common areas, though thankfully rooms are more neutral and sleek.

Rooms with a View

Sweeping panoramas and more intimate scenes of cobbled piazzas are not hard to find in Rome. In a class of their own are **Hotel dei Gladiatori** *(see p145)*, whose suites and terrace overlook the Colosseum, and the **Hotel Eden** *(see p142)*, with drop-dead skyline views. **Residenza Paolo VI** *(see p149)* offers two suites looking across St Peter's Square.

Quiet Treats

For those who seek a haven from the city bustle, the **Hotel Aventino** and its sister hotels *(see p148)* comprise old villas surrounded by shady gardens. **Hotel Santa Prisca** *(see p148)* is a similar set up, with a lower price tag and fewer personal touches. In the centre, **Hotel Santa Maria in Trastevere's** *(see p149)* thick walls keep out any noise from the street.

choice stays

Worth a Splurge

For a 21st-century version of Roman Holiday, **Hotel De Russie** *(see p142)* embodies understated luxury, while the **Hotel Exedra** *(see p147)* is a more traditional yet stylish choice. **Locanda Cairoli** *(see p141)* shines for its clubhouse atmosphere and subtle mix of contemporary art and antique furniture – along with personal service that's second to none.

Historic Sleeps

Some lovingly restored residences offer a special hotel experience. You can lodge in poet John Keats' room at **Hotel Navona** *(see p140)*, or opt for the **Pantheon View B&B** *(see p140)*, a 14th-century palace. **Hotel Bramante** *(see p148)* was the home of one of Rome's finest Renaissance architects; bare beams and antiques imbue it with old-world charm.

No-Frills Stays

The big hotel makeover doesn't mean the Eternal City is off limits to budget travellers. As well as a few better pensions – **Pensione Panda** *(see p143)* is a real find – and more youth-oriented places like breezy **Hotel Colors** *(see p149)*, options include B&Bs such as **Vacanza Romana** *(see p144)* and apartment rentals like **Casa Smith** *(see p148)*.

Hotels

Hotel Navona *a personal service* `7 E3`
Via dei Sediari 8 • 06 686 4203
» www.hotelnavona.com

Versace-tiled bathrooms, original Renaissance frescoes and a central location on the site of ancient Roman baths make this a unique stay. The Australian owners have overseen its upgrade into an elegant three-star hotel that now has several clusters of adjoining rooms, ideal for families or larger groups. **Moderate**

Albergo del Sole al Biscione *budget* `6 D4`
Via del Biscione 76 • 06 6880 6873
» www.solealbiscione.it

This cheap *albergo* (hotel) is scrupulously clean. Singles are small, but the doubles and triples are all a good size, with white walls, wooden furniture and wrought-iron bedsteads. There are communal terraces, and several rooms are blessed with private outdoor space. Opt for a quieter room at the back. **Cheap**

Hotel dei Portoghesi *pretty views* `6 D1`
Via dei Portoghesi 1 • 06 686 4231
» www.hotelportoghesiroma.com

Breakfast is served on the hotel's charming roof garden, overlooking a medieval tower and Portuguese church. Airy, classically decorated rooms and a superb location make up for the slightly off-hand management. The top-floor suites with private balconies are worth splashing out for. **Moderate**

Pantheon View B&B *opulent B&B* `7 F2`
Via del Seminario 87 • 06 699 0294
» www.pantheonview.it

A good-value B&B in a 14th-century palazzo near the Pantheon is almost too good to be true. The rooms and one suite, with private bathrooms, are small but tastefully decorated, with some original marble and exposed brick. Small private balconies give a glimpse of the Pantheon. Payment by cash only. **Cheap**

Casa di Carlo IV *history for rent* `6 B2`
Via dei Banchi Vecchi 132 • 339 214 2009
» www.dolceroma.it

The plaque outside this apartment states that Charles IV of Bohemia stayed here in 1355; the stairwell dates from the same century. Within are two doubles, a bathroom, a kitchen and a dining-lounge area. The minimum stay is three nights. If this place is booked, ask the owners if their studio in Monti is free. **Moderate**

Hotel Art *old school, new style*   `4 C2`
Via Margutta 56 • 06 328 711
>> www.hotelart.it

This cutting-edge designer hotel inhabits half of the Collegio San Giuseppe building, Rome's most exclusive private school. The foyer, once the school chapel, is now a bar-restaurant, which still has a lapis-blue ceiling, the original marble altar and Venetian paving stones, although the furniture is more modern. Two Plexiglas bubbles house the reception and concierge desks. Lime, electric blue, tangerine and fire-engine red define the communal spaces, but the bedrooms, while equally contemporary, are more neutrally decorated, with dark leather headboards and parquet floors. In the rooms, sensors turn the lights on as you enter, and there is access to the Internet through the TV. The basement includes a sauna, a Turkish bath and a small gym. The courtyard is brightened by vibrant 1960s-style plastic chairs. **Expensive**

Locanda Cairoli *luxurious but homely*   `7 E5`
Piazza Benedetto Cairoli 2 • 06 6880 9278
>> www.locandacairoli.it

Your on-site host, an architect who dreamed of creating a welcoming hotel for business travellers, took over the *piano nobile* on the second floor of this 17th-century palazzo, which overlooks the public gardens. All 15 rooms have navy-and-white decor and terracotta floors, but the original contemporary artworks and antiques vary, giving each its own character. Bathrooms are elegant, with old-fashioned taps and big, fluffy towels. The heart of the *locanda* (inn) is the lounge area, which has huge cream sofas, magazines and a clubhouse feel. Generous breakfasts are served at a long communal table. The staff are professional – discreet but cordial. Airport pick-ups, personal shoppers, in-room hairdressing, butlers and night visits to museums can all be arranged. Other thoughtful touches include free newspapers and fully equipped kitchen for out-of-hours snacking. **Expensive**

Hotels

Hotel Eden *caters for every whim* `4 D2`
Via Ludovisi 49 • 06 478 121
» www.hotel-eden.it

Royalty, celebrities and poets have stayed at this little piece of paradise. Extravagance and opulence abound, and the staff give the impression that even the most outlandish request would be satisfied. Rooms are formal, with lavish bathrooms, two TVs and all creature comforts. **Expensive**

Hotel de Russie *real class* `4 C1`
Via del Babuino 9 • 06 328 881
» www.hotelderussie.it

Exuding understated elegance, this historic building is a luxurious urban retreat. Rooms come equipped with an entertainment system and overlook either Piazza del Popolo or the terraced garden that backs on to Villa Borghese. A state-of-the-art gym and health spa *(see p133)* complete the classy package. **Expensive**

Casa Howard *be their guest* `4 D3`
Via Capo le Case 18 • 06 6992 4555
» www.casahoward.com

This tiny oasis of calm has just five stylish rooms. The White Room boasts a dreamy four-poster bed, while the Chinese Room exudes warmth and exoticism. Only two have en-suite bathrooms; the others have private ones down the hall. (Kimonos and slippers are provided.) The hotel's Turkish bath is a bonus. **Moderate**

Hotel Booking Services
You can book most hotels through the free **Hotel Reservation Service** by phone (06 699 1000; multilingual operators available 7am–10pm daily), online (www.hotelreservation.it) or in person at both airports and at Stazione Termini. Otherwise, try the private, independent tourist office **Enjoy Rome** (06 445 1843, www.enjoyrome.com).

L'Hotel Cinquantatré *a little privacy* `5 E3`
Via di San Basilio 53 • 06 4201 4708
» www.lhotel53.it

An intimate atmosphere prevails in this well-located, narrow, buttercup-coloured building. Guests are encouraged to relax on the tiny, top-floor terrace and to indulge in a wonderful spread put on in the breakfast room. Marble bathrooms add to the offerings in this charming hotel. **Moderate**

Hotel Aleph *upmarket, theatrical hotel* `5 E2`
Via di San Basilio 15 • 06 422 901
>> www.boscolohotels.com

Aleph is for those who like bold choices. The dramatic entrance sets the tone: a pair of caged stone lions guard the steps, while huge, masked Samurai warriors dominate the lobby. New York-based designer Adam Tihany drew inspiration from Dante's *Divine Comedy*. Red and black lacquer dominate, accompanied by a rich assortment of velvet and other tactile fabrics. The bar, with its red leather stools, is moved to the top-floor roof terrace in summer and attracts the rich and beautiful. Tempting Mediterranean morsels are on offer at in-house restaurant Sin, where wine is served in ruby-red crystal goblets. The decor is calmer in the bedrooms, where black-and-white photos of Rome stand out from the neutral minimalist surroundings. TVs with wireless keyboards allow in-bed Internet browsing. Alternatively, take a trip to Paradise, the on-site health club, to relax body and mind. **Expensive**

Pensione Panda *an absolute steal* `4 C2`
Via della Croce 35 • 06 678 0179
>> www.hotelpanda.it

Intimate and friendly, this quaint *pensione* in a palazzo has the best price–location ratio in central Rome. The rooms are comfortable and tastefully decorated. Not all are en suite, but the communal bathrooms are immaculate. There are no TVs or air conditioning, and breakfast costs extra. **Cheap**

Residenza Frattina *peace and quiet* `4 D3`
Via Frattina 104 • 06 678 3553
>> www.residenzafrattinacorso.com

Step out of this tranquil nine-room hotel and you're in the heart of Rome's shopping district. Full of antiques and character, Frattina offers comfortable, classically furnished rooms. It also has a suite that makes clever use of a very narrow space. Breakfast is served in the rose-pink lounge bar. **Moderate**

A Heavenly Sleep
Some religious institutions accept paying guests. Most have early curfews (10–11pm), and some are single-sex. Try the peaceful **Franciscan Sisters of Atonement** close to St Peter's; the central **Nostra Signora di Lourdes**; or the **Casa di Santa Brigida**, which has three residences (but no curfews) across the city. For further details of all, *see p185*.

Hotels

Hotel Locarno *original style* `4 B2`
Via della Penna 22 • 06 361 0841
>> www.hotellocarno.com

With its Tiffany lamps in the bar and the antique coffee-maker in the restaurant, this 1925 hotel is delightful. Each room is unique, and most have period fittings and all mod cons. Those in the new wing are generally smarter and include superior doubles as well as suites with huge bathrooms. **Moderate**

Hotel Parlamento *a quiet refuge* `7 F1`
Via delle Convertite 5 • 06 6992 1000
>> www.hotelparlamento.it

This friendly, labyrinthine hotel offers small but pretty pastel-coloured rooms. Room 108 sleeps four and has a balcony. Three more-expensive rooms include terraces and Jacuzzis. Breakfast is flexible in both time and location – in your room, downstairs or on the roof garden. Air conditioning costs extra. **Moderate**

Hostel des Artistes *cheerful hostel* `5 H2`
Via Villafranca 20 • 06 445 4365
>> www.hostelrome.com

The young owners of the three-star Hotel des Artistes reserve one floor for this hostel, which offers singles through to quintuples, as well as dorm beds. It's handy for Termini and all rooms are clean and airy, with fans, safes and satellite TVs. Breakfast can be taken in the Hotel des Artistes for a 12€ supplement. **Cheap**

B&B Vacanze Romane *B&B with flair* `5 G4`
Via Carlo Alberto 26
06 444 1079

The owners' passion for collecting film memorabilia and antique toys gives this spot its character. The three good-sized double and triple rooms share two bathrooms and a pleasant entrance. The B&B also has an annexe, with three high-ceilinged en-suite rooms. Breakfast is served at a bar down the road. **Cheap**

Bed and Breakfasts

B&Bs are a relatively recent phenomenon in Rome, created to cope with the influx of Catholic pilgrims during the year 2000. After the initial flurry, only the committed remain in the market, be they pleasant private homes in the suburbs or Renaissance palazzos in the centre. Italian B&Bs are often annexes to family homes, so although there's no home-cooked breakfast (hygiene laws forbid it), you do get privacy. The **Chamber of Commerce,** which vets all Rome's B&Bs, has the most comprehensive website (www.bedroma.com), listing around 400 establishments. Agencies such as the **B&B Association of Rome** (www.b-b.rm.it) and **Enjoy Rome** (www.enjoy rome.com) provide smaller, more manageable selections.

Residenza Monti *well-placed studios* `5 E5`
Via dei Serpenti 15 • 06 481 5736
>> www.therelaxinghotels.com

Step off the busy and bohemian streets of the Monti quarter into this peaceful palazzo. The apartments and studios are simply decorated, with pleasant, smallish rooms and, in some cases, attic rooms. Prices are very affordable, but the proprietors prefer to have guests on longer lets than short breaks. **Moderate**

Antica Locanda *affordable gem* `5 E4`
Via del Boschetto 84 • 06 484 894
>> www.antica-locanda.com

A jewel in an old palazzo, Antica Locanda has bare beams, iron beds and somewhat old-fashioned decor in the rooms, which are named after famous composers and artists. Its pretty roof garden overlooks Roman ruins and makes a lovely summer refuge. The hotel's friendly owners run the tavern below. **Moderate**

Hotel Villa delle Rose *eastern wonder* `5 G3`
Via Vicenza 5 • 06 445 1788
>> www.villadellerose.it

This once rather run-down hotel, close to hectic Termini, may have been given a face-lift, but it still retains an informal atmosphere, and the double-glazed windows will ensure a peaceful night's sleep. The delightful rose garden provides a welcome respite after a day's sightseeing. **Moderate**

Hotel dei Gladiatori *ancient vistas* `9 G1`
Via Labicana 125 • 06 7759 1380
>> www.hotelgladiatori.it

Check into a suite here and you'll see the Colosseum from your bath or bed. Take a normal room and the view of the Ludus Magnus – the gladiators' changing rooms – is still impressive. The decor is inspired by ancient Rome, with mosaics and faux classical motifs. A sunset apéritif on the terrace is divine. **Moderate**

Hotel Piemonte *given an update* `5 G3`
Via Vicenza 34a • 06 445 2240
>> www.hotelpiemonte.com

The Piemonte is one of many hotels in this area that was transformed before the year 2000 to become a comfortable, fully equipped three-star; it now has air con, Internet access and smart decor. The en-suite rooms are a good size, if rather formally decorated. Staff are professional and helpful. **Moderate**

Radisson SAS ES.Hotel *style city* `5 H5`

Via Filippo Turati 171 • 06 444 841
>> www.rome.radissonsas.com

The only purpose-built hotel in the historic centre, the Radisson was constructed over the remains of a Roman road – still visible under the foyer – which was the inspiration for some details in the design by dynamic Anglo-Italian architects King & Rosselli. The hotel is the epitome of contemporary style and a favourite setting for fashion and film shoots, as well as the hotel of choice for the rich and the glamorous, including models, film stars, directors, architects and designers. The rooms combine minimalism with luxury and warmth; modular furniture moulds together the bed, shower, sink and wardrobe into one movable, changeable unit. All the suites are individually designed, some targeting specific needs, such as the fitness suite, which has a small gym area in the room and on the private terrace. A bedside console in all the rooms and suites allows guests to control the temperature, lights and blinds, as well as the flat-screen TV and DVD. Lampshades of spinnaker cloth expand into translucent balloons with the warmth of halogen lamps. The flooring ranges from parquetry in the suites to comfortable foam-backed PVC in the rooms. In the library, guests can relax on leather sofas, browse the eclectic range of art and photography books and sip some bubbly. The hotel gym is large, with state-of-the-art machines, and there's an attached spa. An inviting pool on the roof adjoins the innovative Sette restaurant *(see p38)* and the sleek cocktail bar Zest *(see p116)*. The service doesn't always live up to expectation, but it's the aesthetic that's the draw. **Expensive**

Hotel Exedra *worth the splurge* `5 F3`
Piazza della Repubblica 47 • 06 489 381
>> www.boscolohotels.com

From the glass-floored meeting rooms set over Roman ruins to the top-floor pool, the Exedra successfully mixes the old with the new. Everything is big: the high atrium, the corridors, the rooms. Many of the guest rooms – classy and neutral, with lavish bathrooms – have views of Piazza della Repubblica. **Expensive**

Hotel Capo d'Africa *modish living* `9 G1`
Via Capo d'Africa 54 • 06 772 801
>> www.hotelcapodafrica.com

Serious contemporary art and sleek design characterize this former school, which has been transformed into a modern five-star hotel. Rooms are large with high ceilings, and have direct Internet connections. There's a well-equipped gym and a breakfast-bar terrace overlooking the Colosseum. **Expensive**

Hotel Lancelot *warm and welcoming* `9 G1`
Via Capo d'Africa 47 • 06 7045 0615
>> www.lancelothotel.com

The staff at this elegant hotel make it a real home from home. Tucked away in a quiet street, the Lancelot offers uncluttered rooms (two of which have disabled access). The communal areas – a vine-covered patio and an inviting lounge – are conducive to quiet reading or intimate conversation. Half-board available. **Moderate**

Forty Seven *stylish home from home* `9 E1`
Via Petroselli 47 • 06 678 7816
>> www.fortysevenhotel.com

Each of this hotel's five floors is dedicated to a 20th-century Italian artist, with original prints adorning the walls of the comfortable bedrooms. The sinuous lines and understated design echoes the Art Deco period from which the building dates. The rooftop terrace is the perfect spot for a sundowner. **Expensive**

Hotel Abitart *theme nights* `10 C3`
Via Matteucci 10–12 • 06 454 3191
>> abitart.hotel-roma.net

The only hotel in the up-and-coming Ostiense area has eight art-inspired suites. A print of *Guernica* dominates the Picasso Suite; the Keith Haring Suite is a riot of colour; and the Photographic Suite's walls are printed with grainy black-and-white images. Several rooms are suitable for wheelchairs. **Moderate**

Hotels

Hotel Aventino *sumptuous surroundings* `8 D3`
Via San Domenico 10 • 06 578 3214
>> www.aventinohotels.com

The cool and quiet of Aventino, one of Rome's most sought-after residential areas, makes this a very tempting proposal, especially in summer, when you can enjoy a generous buffet breakfast on wicker chairs in the courtyard. The rooms in this carefully renovated old villa are warm and inviting. **Moderate**

Hotel Santa Prisca *a holy haven* `8 D4`
Largo Manlio Gelsomini
25 06 574 1917

Close to bustling Testaccio, Santa Prisca is a quiet, if slightly institutional, hotel owned (but not run) by an order of nuns. The rooms are small and simply decorated, and there's plenty of green space in the hotel's grounds for relaxing. A large free parking area makes it perfect if you're travelling by car. **Cheap**

Hotel Bramante *ancient urbanism* `1 C3`
Vicolo delle Palline 24 • 06 6880 6426
>> www.hotelbramante.com

This historic inn, tucked behind the wall that links the Vatican with Castel Sant'Angelo, was once home to Renaissance architect Domenico Fontana. He would no doubt approve of the impeccable restoration of the 16 serene rooms, all furnished with antiques. The breakfast table is generously laden. **Moderate**

Casa Smith *palazzo for hire* `8 B3`
Piazza Ippolito Nievo 1
06 581 5580

Casa Smith is a stylishly furnished home with a fully equipped galley kitchen, a double bedroom and a lounge that comes with a piano and a second, fold-down double bed. Fresh milk, fruit and croissants are provided for breakfast. In the same palazzo, two charming studio flats are suitable for couples. **Cheap**

Apartment Rental

Holiday apartments, known as *case vacanze*, are an increasingly popular choice with switched-on travellers. The types of property and services available and minimum stay required vary greatly. *Case* are particularly good for families with young children, and large groups. Apartments are for rent all over the city, but the more central a place is, the more expensive it's likely to be. With improved public transport, though, being outside the centre isn't such a setback. Many of the same agencies deal both in B&Bs (*see p144*) and apartment rentals. The house owners often network among themselves, so if the place you want to stay in is booked, the owner may well give you other leads. (*See **Casa Smith**, above, **Casa di Carlo IV**, p140, and **Residenza Monti**, p145.*)

Hotel Santa Maria in Trastevere

8 C1

Vicolo del Piede 2 • 06 589 4626
>> www.hotelsantamaria.info

This ex-convent is a rare oasis of calm in Trastevere. Its ancient walls protect you from the noise of night revellers wending their way down cobbled streets. The original structure has been retained, so rooms are on the small side. However, they are welcoming and immaculately clean, with light wood, terracotta and warm yellow hues, together with country-style bed covers. Each one is built around the courtyard and faces on to the garden of orange trees. Not only is breakfast served here, but it also makes an ideal spot for recovering from a day's sightseeing with a bottle of *prosecco* (sparkling wine) before heading out to dinner.

The suites under the eaves are charming, but the upstairs bedrooms are awkward for tall people. One room is suitable for wheelchair-users. The service is personal and the staff are keen to help you discover the best of Rome. **Moderate**

Residenza Paolo VI   *the best in the west*   1 C3

Via Paolo VI 29 • 06 6813 4108
>> www.residenzapaolovi.com

If the Vatican is the focus of your trip, this monastery-turned-four-star-hotel is for you. A superb communal terrace looks past the colonnade straight into the Papal palace. Two junior suites share the same view. Housed in the original monks' quarters, double rooms are small but elegantly furnished. **Moderate**

Hotel Colors   *easy on the pocket*   1 D2

Via Boezio 31 • 06 687 4030
>> www.colorshotel.com

This top-floor hostel offers everything a budget traveller could wish for – except a lift. The rooms are each painted a different colour, some share bathrooms and there's a cheery, clean dorm that sleeps five. You can rustle up your own breakfast in the kitchen and enjoy a beer on the terrace. **Cheap**

The heart of modern Rome is encompassed by the
seven hills that defined the ancient city. The suburbs
extend well beyond them, but most of this guide's
recommendations lie within the ancient Roman walls
in a compact and easily walkable area. Almost every
listing in this guide features a page and grid reference
to the maps in this section. The few entries that fall
outside the area covered by these maps have
transport details instead. The main map below shows
the division of the Street Finder, along with names.
An index of the street names follows on *pp163–7*.

Greater Rome

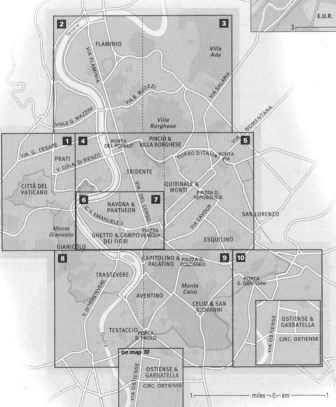

Key to Street Finder

- Sight/public building
- Ⓜ Metro station
- Ⓢ Railway station
- Main bus stop
- Ⓣ Tram terminus
- ⓘ Tourist information office
- Ⓗ Hospital with casualty unit
- Ⓟ Police station
- Church
- Ⓢ Synagogue
- Ⓧ Post office
- Ⓟ Car park
- Railway line
- Pedestrian street

Scale of maps 1–5 and 8–10

| 0 metres | 400 |
| 0 yards | 400 |

Scale of maps 6–7

| 0 metres | 200 |
| 0 yards | 200 |

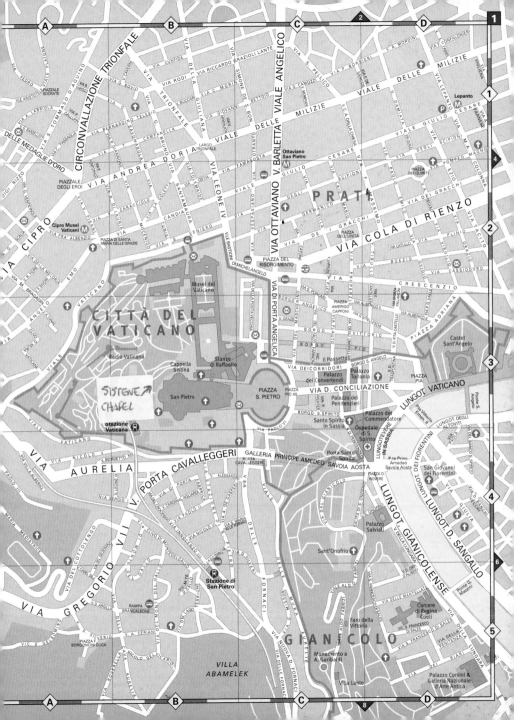

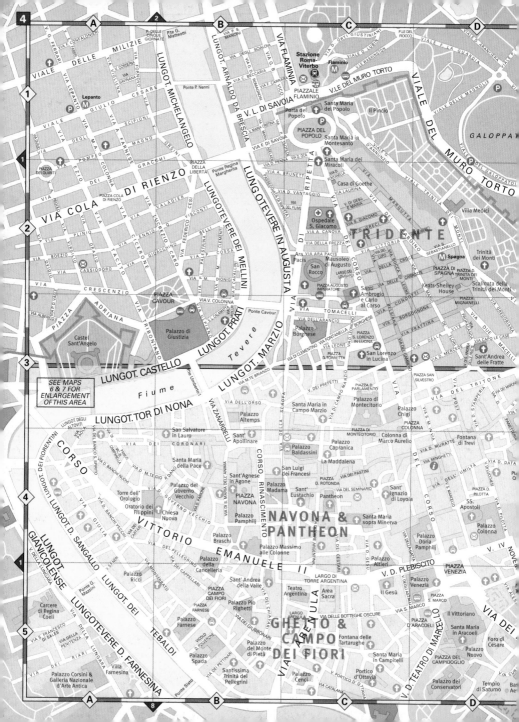

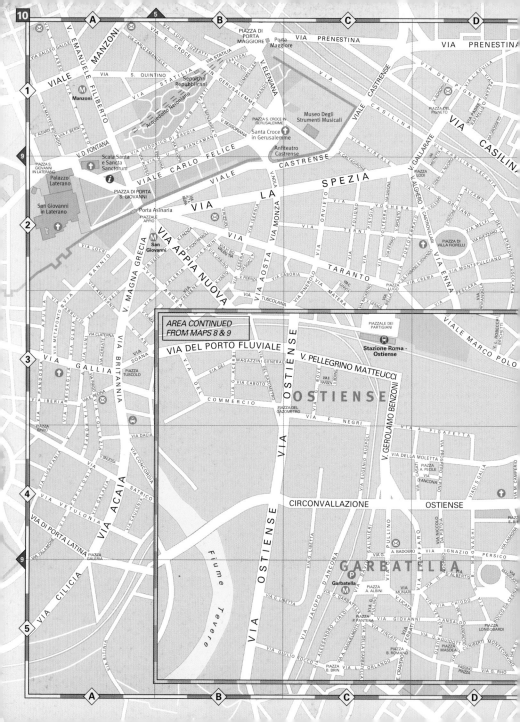

Index of Selected Streets

Index of Selected Streets

Amore e Psiche (p70)
Via Santa Caterina da Siena 61
(Map 7 F3) 06 678 3908
Books

Arsenale (p52)
Via del Governo Vecchio 64
(Map 6 F3) 06 686 1380
Women's clothes

Bottega Veneta (p53)
Piazza San Lorenzo in Lucina
11–13 (Map 4 C3)
Accessories

Campo Marzio Design (p57)
Via di Campo Marzio 41
(Map 4 C3)
Pens

Enoteca al Parlamento (p64)
Via dei Prefetti 15 (Map 7 E1)
Food & drink

**Enoteca di Sardegna
Pigna** (p60)
Via della Pigna 3a (Map 7 F3)
Food & drink

Ferrari Store (p53)
Via Tomacelli 147 (Map 4 C3)
Branded Ferrari products

Galleria d'Arte Sacra (p57)
Via dei Cestari 15
(Map 7 E3)
Religious objects

Giorgi & Febbi (p57)
Piazza della Rotonda 61–2
(Map 7 E2)
Interiors

Maga Morgana (p53)
Via del Governo Vecchio 27 &
98 (Map 6 C3)
Women's clothes

Marmi Line (p52)
Via dei Coronari 141–5
(Map 6 C2)
Classical statuary

Modavì (p59)
Via di Campo Marzio 10c
(Map 7 E1)
Accessories

Pro Fumum Durante (p60)
Via della Colonna Antonina 27
(Map 7 F2)
Beauty

Retrò (p56)
Piazza del Fico 20–21
(Map 6 C2)
Vintage & second-hand

SBU (p53)
Via di San Pantaleo 68
(Map 6 D3)
Men's clothes

Ta Matete (p70)
Via della Pilotta 16
(Map 4 D4)
Books

Le Tartarughe (p52)
Via Piè di Marmo 17 (Map 7 F3)
Via Piè di Marmo 33 (Map 7 F3)
Via del Gesù 71a (Map 7 F3)
Women's clothes

Art & Architecture

Ghetto & Campo dei Fiori

**Area Sacra di Largo
Argentina** (p79)
(Map 7 E4)
Ancient site

Galleria Spada (p79)
Palazzo Spada, Piazza Capo
di Ferro
(Map 6 D5)
Gallery

Isola Tiberina (p80)
(Map 8 D1)
Island

Museo Crypta Balbi (p78)
Via delle Botteghe Oscure 31
(Map 7 F4)
Museum

Museo d'Arte Ebraica (p124)
Lungotevere dei Cenci
(Map 8 D1)
Museum

Palazzo Farnese (p90)
Piazza Farnese
(Map 6 C4)
Palace

Sant'Andrea della Valle (p79)
Corso Vittorio Emanuele II 6
(Map 6 D4)
Church

San Bartolomeo (p80)
Isola Tiberina (Map 8 D1)
Church

Synagogue (p124)
Lungotevere dei Cenci
(Map 8 D1)
Synagogue

Tartarughe (p86)
Piazza Mattei (Map 7 E5)
Fountain

Navona & Pantheon

Chiostro del Bramante (p76)
Vicolo dell'Arco
della Pace (Map 6 D2)
Church

**Column of Marcus
Aurelius** (p80)
Piazza Colonna (Map 7 F1)
Monument

Galleria Doria Pamphilj (p78)
Palazzo Doria, Piazza del
Collegio Romano 2 (Map 7 G3)
Gallery

Il Gesù (p78)
Piazza del Gesù (Map 7 F4)
Church

Museo di Roma (p77)
Palazzo Braschi, Via di San
Pantaleo 10 (Map 6 D3)
Museum

Palazzo Altemps (p76)
Piazza Sant'Apollinare 48
(Map 6 D1)
Museum

Palazzo Chigi (p80)
Piazza Colonna (Map 7 F1)
Palace

Pantheon (p13, p77)
Piazza Rotonda (Map 7 E2)
Church

Quattro Fiumi (p86)
Piazza Navona (Map 6 D2)
Fountain

Sant'Agnese in Agone (p76)
Piazza Navona
(Map 6 D2)
Church

Sant'Agostino (p77)
Piazza Sant'Agostino (Map 6 D2)
Church

Sant'Ignazio (p87)
Piazza di S. Ignazio (Map 7 F2)
Church

San Lorenzo in Lucina (p91)
Via in Lucina 16a (Map 7 F1)
Church

San Luigi dei Francesi (p79)
Via San Giovanna d'Arco
(Map 6 D2)
Church

Santa Maria della Pace (p76)
Vicolo dell'Arco della Pace
(Map 6 C2)
Church

**Santa Maria Sopra
Minerva** (p77)
Piazza della Minerva (Map 7 F3)
Church

Via del Corso (p80)
(Map 4 C3)
Ancient site

Performance

Ghetto & Campo dei Fiori

Cinema Teatro-Farnese (p101)
Piazza Campo dei Fiori 56
(Map 6 D4)
Cinema

Rialto Sant'Ambrogio (p132)
Via Sant'Ambrogio 4
(Map 7 F5)
Centro sociale

Rinascita (p107)
Via delle Botteghe Oscure 1–5
(Map 7 F4) 06 6992 2436
Ticket outlet

Teatro Argentina (p100)
Largo Argentina 52
(Map 7 E4)
Multi-function venue

Navona & Pantheon

Modo (p100)
Vicolo del Fico 3 (Map 6 C2)
Jazz venue

Ricordi (p107)
Via del Corso 506 (Map 4 C2)
06 320 2790
Ticket outlet

Teatro Valle (p101)
Via del Teatro Valle 21
(Map 7 E3)
Theatre

» **€ cheap**   **€€ moderate**   **€€€ expensive**   (Price ranges: Restaurants, *see p29*, Hotels, *see p141*)

Index by Area

Centre

Bars & Clubs

Ghetto & Campo dei Fiori

Crudo (p112)
Via degli Specchi 6 (Map 7 E5)
Bar

Il Nolano (p113)
Piazza Campo dei Fiori 11–12
(Map 6 D4)
Bar

La Vineria (p112)
Piazza Campo dei Fiori 15
(Map 6 C4)
Bar

Navona & Pantheon

Anima (p113)
Via Santa Maria dell'Anima 57
(Map 6 D2)
Club

Bar del Fico (p112)
Piazza del Fico 26
(Map 6 C2)
Bar

Caffè della Pace (p113)
Via della Pace 3–7
(Map 6 C2)
Bar

Ciampini (p119)
Piazza San Lorenzo in Lucina
29 (Map 4 C3)
06 687 6606
Bar

Enoteca il Piccolo (p113)
Via del Governo Vecchio 74–5
(Map 6 C3)
Bar

La Maison (p114)
Vicolo dei Granari 4
(Map 6 D3)
Club

Raphael Hotel (p119)
Largo Febo 2 (Map 6 D2)
06 682 831
www.raphaelhotel.com
Bar

Supperclub (p114)
Via dei Nari 14 (Map 7 E3)
Club

Trinity College (p39, p120)
Via del Collegio Romano 6
(Map 7 G2)
06 678 6472
Pub

Hotels

Ghetto & Campo dei Fiori

**Albergo del Sole al
Biscione** (p140)   €
Via del Biscione 76
(Map 6 D4)

Casa di Carlo IV (p140)   €€
Via dei Banchi Vecchi 132
(Map 6 B2)

Casa di Santa Brigida (p143) €
Piazza Farnese 96
(Map 6 C4)
06 6889 2596

Locanda Cairoli (p141)   €€
Piazza Benedetto Cairoli 2
(Map 7 E5)

Navona & Pantheon

Hotel dei Portoghesi (p140)€€
Via dei Portoghesi 1
(Map 6 D1)

Hotel Navona (p140)   €
Via dei Sediari 8
(Map 7 E3)

Pantheon View B&B (p140) €
Via del Seminario 87
(Map 7 F2)

North

Restaurants

Northern Suburbs/
Flaminio & Olimpico

ReD (p126)   €€
Viale Pietro de Coubertin 30
(Map 2 D2) 06 8069 1630
Roman

Pincio & Villa Borghese

Le Bistrot d'Hubert (p36) €€
Via Sardegna 135 (Map 5 F1)
French

Mangiamoci (p34)   €€
Salita di San Sebastianello
(Map 4 D2)
International

Tridente

Buccone (p65)   €
Via di Ripetta 19–20 (Map 4 C2)
Enoteca

Da Settimio all'Arancio (p37)   €€
Via dell'Arancio 50 (Map 4 C3)
Italian

'Gusto (p35, p39, p64)   €€
Piazza Augusto Imperatore 9
(Map 4 C2)
Enoteca/Italian/Pizza

Il Margutta Ristorarte (p34) €€
Via Margutta 118 (Map 4 C2)
Vegetarian

Le Pain Quotidien (p37)   €
Via Tomacelli 24–5
(Map 4 C3)
Baked goods

Pizza Rè (p36)   €
Via di Ripetta 14 (Map 4 C2)
Pizza

Shopping

Northern Suburbs/Trieste

Brooks (p65)
Via Tarvisio 4 (Ⓜ Bologna)
06 841 3653
High-street fashion

Pincio & Villa Borghese

Fausto Santini (p62)
Via Frattina 120
(Map 4 D3)
Shoes

Michel Harem (p61)
Via Sistina 137a (Map 5 E3)
Vintage & second-hand

Tridente

Abitart (p66)
Via della Croce 46–7
(Map 4 C2)
Women's clothes

Alberta Ferretti (p61)
Via Condotti 34 (Map 4 C3)
International designer

Alinari (p65)
Via Alibert 16a (Map 4 D2)
Prints & photos

Anglo-American Book Co (p70)
Via della Vite 102
(Map 4 D3)
06 679 5222
Books

Armani (p61)
Via Condotti 77 (Map 4 C3)
www.giorgioarmani.com
International designer

Avant (p65)
Via del Corso 77 (Map 4 C2)
06 228 0104
High-street fashion

Benetton (p65)
Via del Corso 422–3
(Map 4 D2)
06 6810 2520
High-street fashion

Buccellati (p63)
Via Condotti 31 (Map 4 D3)
Accessories

Buccone (p36, p65)
Via di Ripetta 19 (Map 4 C2)
Food & drink

Bulgari (p62)
Via Condotti 10 (Map 4 D2)
Accessories

Cravattterie Nazionali (p63)
Via Vittoria 62 (Map 4 C2)
Accessories

D&G (p61)
Piazza di Spagna 93–6
(Map 4 D2)
www.dolcegabbana.it
International designer

Il Discount dell'Alta Moda (p66)
Via di Gesù e Maria 14–16a
(Map 4 C2)
Men's & women's clothes

Dolce & Gabbana (p61)
Via Condotti 52 (Map 4 D2)
www.dolcegabbana.it
International designer

Emporio Libreria Gusto
(p35, p64)
Piazza Augusto Imperatore 7
(Map 4 C2)
Food & drink

Ermenegildo Zegna (p61)
Via Borgognona 7e (Map 4 C3)
www.ermenegildozegna.it
International designer

Fendi (p61)
Via Borgognona 36–40
(Map 4 C3) www.fendi.it
International designer

Ferragamo (p61)
Via Condotti 73–4 (Map 4 C3)
www.ferragamo.com
International designer

Francesco Biasia (p66)
Via Due Macelli 62–62a
(Map 4 D3)
Accessories

Frette (p61)
Piazza di Spagna 11 (Map 4 D2)
www.frette.it
International designer

Gucci (p61)
Via Borgognona 7d
(Map 4 C3)
Via Condotti 68a
(Map 4 C3)
Via Condotti 8
(Map 4 C3)
www.gucci.com
International designer

Libreria Francesco Ponti (p64)
Via Tomacelli 23 (Map 4 C3)
Books

Lion Bookshop (p70)
Via dei Greci 33–6 (Map 4 C2)
06 3265 4007
Books

Luisella Mariotti (p64)
Via di Gesù e Maria 20a
(Map 4 C2)
Accessories

Mandarina Duck (p61)
Via dei Due Macelli 59
(Map 4 D3)
Accessories

Mariella Burani (p61)
Via Bocca di Leone 28
(Map 4 C2)
International designer

Missoni (p61)
Piazza di Spagna 78 (Map 4 D2)
www.missoni.it
International designer

Modigliani (p61)
Via Condotti 24 (Map 4 D2)
Interiors

Moschino (p61)
Via Borgognona 32a
(Map 4 C3)
www.moschino.it
International designer

Nostalgica (p63)
Via di Ripetta 30–1
(Map 4 C2)
Retro soccer kits

Onyx (p61)
Via del Corso 132
(Map 4 C3)
Women's clothes

La Perla (p65)
Via Condotti 79 (Map 4 D2)
Lingerie

Prada (p61)
Via Condotti 91 (Map 4 C3)
www.prada.com
International designer

La Rinascente (p65)
Largo Chigi 20 (Map 7 G1)
06 679 7691
Department store

Schostal (p64)
Via del Corso 158
(Map 4 C2) 06 679 1240
Accessories

Sergio Rossi (p61)
Piazza di Spagna 97–100
(Map 4 D2)
www.sergiorossi.com
International designer

Simona (p63)
Via del Corso 82–3 (Map 4 C2)
Lingerie

Sisley (p65)
Via del Corso 413–15
(Map 4 D2)
Via Condotti 59 (Map 4 C3)
www.sisley.com
High-street fashion

Sportstaff (p65)
Piazza di Spagna 84–5
(Map 4 D2) 06 678 1599
High-street fashion

Stefanel (p65)
Via Frattina 31–32 (Map 4 D3)
Via del Corso 123 (Map 4 C3)
www.stefanel.it
High-street fashion

TAD (p62)
Via del Babuino 155a (Map 4 C2)
Concept store

Valentino (p61)
Via del Babuino 61 (Map 4 C2)
Via Condotti 13 (Map 4 C3)
Via Bocca di Leone 15–16
(Map 4 C2)
www.valentino.it
International designer

Versace (p61, p180)
Via Borgognona 24–5
(Map 4 C3)
Via Bocca di Leone 26–7
(Map 4 C2)
www.versace.com
International designer

Xandrine (p66)
Via della Croce 88 (Map 4 C2)
Women's clothes

Yamamay (p64)
Via Frattina 86 (Map 4 C3)
Lingerie

Art & Architecture

Northern Suburbs/ Flaminio & Olimpico

British School (p85)
Via Antonio Gramsci 61
(Map 2 D4) www.bsr.ac.uk
Exhibition space

MAXXI (p83)
Via Guido Reni 10 (Map 2 B2)
Gallery

Santa Croce (p91)
Piazza di Santa Croce in
Gerusalemme (Map 10 B1)
Church

Pincio & Villa Borghese

Fontana delle Api (p84)
Piazza Barberini (Map 5 E3)
Fountain

Galleria Borghese (p13, p84)
Villa Borghese (Map 3 F5)
Gallery

Galleria Nazionale d'Arte Antica (p84)
Palazzo Barberini, Piazza
Barberini (Map 5 E3)
Gallery

Galleria Nazionale d'Arte Moderna (p85)
Viale delle Belle Arti 131
(Map 3 E5) 06 322 981
Gallery

Keats-Shelley Memorial House (p85)
Piazza di Spagna 26 (Map 4 D2)
Museum

MACRO (p83)
Via Reggio Emilia 54
(Map 5 G1)
Gallery

Museo Hendrik Christian Anderson (p83)
Via Pasquale Stanislao
Mancini 20 (Map 4 B1)
Museum

Museo Nazionale di Villa Giulia (p127)
Piazzale di Villa Giulia 9
(Map 2 D5) 06 322 6571
Museum

Palazzo Barberini (p84)
Piazza Barberini (Map 5 E3)
Palace

Piazza Barberini (p84)
(Map 5 E3)
Square

Santa Maria della Concezione (p84)
Piazza Barberini (Map 5 E3)
Church

Spanish Steps (p15, p81)
(Map 4 D2)

Trinità dei Monti (p81)
Piazza della Trinità dei Monti
(Map 4 D2)
Church

Il Tritone (p84)
Piazza Barberini
(Map 5 E3)
Fountain

>> € cheap   €€ moderate   €€€ expensive   (Price ranges: Restaurants, *see p29*, Hotels, *see p141*)

Index by Area

North

East

Colline Emiliane (p38)   €€
Via degli Avignonesi 22
(Map 5 E3)
Emilia-Romagnan

Costantini (p36)   €€
Piazza Cavour 16
(Map 4 B2) 06 321 3210
Enoteca

**Est! Est!! Est!!! –
Da Ricci** (p39)   €
Via Genova 32 (Map 5 F4)
Pizza

F.I.S.H. (p41)   €€
Via dei Serpenti 16
(Map 5 E5)
Seafood

San Crispino (p30)   €
Via della Panetteria 42
(Map 7 H1)
06 7045 0412
Ice cream

Sora Lucia (p37)   €
Via della Panetteria 41a
(Map 7 H1)
Italian

San Lorenzo

Arancia Blu (p40)   €€
Via dei Latini 55–65
(Map 6 F4)
Vegetarian

Il Dito e la Luna (p41)   €€
Via dei Sabelli 51
(Bus Nos. 71, 204, 492)
Sicilian

Hostaria degli Artisti (p38)   €
Via Germano Sommeiller 6
(Map 10 B1)
Neapolitan

Uffa Che Pizza (p38)   €
Via dei Taurini 39
(Tram lines 3, 19 to Reti)
Pizza

Shopping

Eastern Suburbs/
Prenestino

Goodfellas (p69)
Circonvallazione Casilina 44
(Tram to Lodi)
Music

Esquilino

Feltrinelli International (p70)
Via Vittorio Emanuele Orlando
78–81 (Map 5 F3)
06 487 0171
Books

MAS (p65, p128, p180)
Via dello Statuto 11 (Map 5 G5)
Department store

Panella, L'Arte del Pane (p69)
Largo Leopardi 2 (Map 5 G5)
Food & drink

Trimani Enoteca (p68)
Via Goito 20
(Map 5 G2)
Food & drink

Quirinale & Monti

Fiorucci (p69)
Via Nazionale 236
(Map 5 F3)
Women's clothes

Le Gallinelle (p67)
Via del Boschetto 76
(Map 5 E4)
Vintage & second-hand

LOL (p67)
Piazza degli Zingari 11
(Map 5 F5)
Women's clothes

Maurizio de Nisi (p68)
Via Panisperna 51
(Map 5 E4)
Vintage & second-hand

Pulp (p67)
Via del Boschetto 140
(Map 5 E5)
Vintage & second-hand

La Vetrata di Passagrilli (p68)
Via del Boschetto 94
(Map 5 E5)
Glassware

San Lorenzo

Disfunzioni Musicali (p69)
Via degli Etruschi 4
(Tram to Lodi)
Music

Art & Architecture

Esquilino

Museo Nazionale Romano (p86)
Palazzo Massimo alle Terme:
Largo di Villa Peretti 1
06 3996 7700
(Map 5 G3)
Aula Ottagonale: Via Parigi
(Map 5 G3)
Terme di Diocleziano: Via de
Nicola (Map 5 G3)
06 3996 7700
Museum

Santa Maria della Vittoria (p78)
Via XX Settembre 17
(Map 5 F3)
Church

Santa Maria Maggiore (p93)
Piazza di Santa Maria
Maggiore (Map 5 G4)
Church

San Pietro in Vincoli
(p90, p91)
Piazza di San Pietro in Vincoli
(Map 5 F5)
Church

Quirinale & Monti

Fontana di Trevi (p15, p86)
(Map 7 G1)
Fountain

Palazzo del Quirinale (p85)
Piazza Monte Cavallo
(Map 5 E4)
Palace

Sant'Andrea al Quirinale (p85)
Via del Quirinale (Map 5 E3)
Church

**San Carlo alle Quattro
Fontane** (p85)
Via del Quirinale (Map 5 E3)
Church

Scuderie del Quirinale (p85)
Via XXIV Maggio 16
(Map 5 E4)
Gallery

San Lorenzo

San Lorenzo Fuori le Mura (p93)
Piazzale del Verano 3
(Tram lines 3, 19 to Reti)
Church

Performance

Eastern Suburbs/
Portonaccio

La Palma (p103)
Via Giuseppe Mirri 35
(Stazione Tiburtina)
Rock & pop venue

Eastern Suburbs/
Prenestino

Forte Prenestino (p99)
Via Federico Delpino
(Train to Centocelle)
06 2180 7855
www.forteprenestino.net
Centro sociale

Esquilino

Lazio Point (p107)
Via Farini 34
(Map 5 G4)
06 482 6688
Football goods store

Orbis (p107)
Piazza dell'Esquilino 37
(Map 5 F4)
06 482 7403
Ticket outlet

Il Posto delle Fragole (p103)
Via Carlo Botta 51
(Map 9 H1)
Multi-function venue

Teatro Ambra Jovinelli (p102)
Via Guglielmo Pepe 43–7
(Map 5 H5)
Comedy

**Teatro dell'Opera di
Roma** (p104)
Piazza Beniamino Gigli 1
(Map 5 F3)
Opera

San Lorenzo

Locanda Atlantide (p117)
Via dei Lucani 22b
(Tram lines 3, 19 to Reti)
Rock & pop venue

Palatine (p89)
Via di San Gregorio 30
(Map 9 E1)
Ancient site

Piazza della Bocca della
Verità (p90)
(Map 9 E1)
Square

Roman Forum (p12, p89)
Enter from Via Sacra, Largo
Romolo e Remo or Via del Foro
Romano
(Map 9 E1)
Ancient site

Santa Maria in
Cosmedin (p90)
Piazza della Bocca della Verita
(Map 9 E1)
Church

Temple of Hercules (p90)
Piazza della Bocca della Verita
(Map 9 E1)
Ancient site

Temple of Portunus (p93)
Piazza della Bocca della Verita
(Map 9 E1)
Ancient site

Celio & San Giovanni

Basilica di San
Clemente (p87)
Via San Giovanni in Laterano
(Map 9 G1)
Church

Casa del Jazz (p103)
Viale di Porta Ardeatina 55
(Map 9 G5)
Jazz venue

Case Romane di San Giovanni
e San Paolo (p88)
Clivo di Scauro (Map 9 G2)
Ancient site

Domus Aurea (p87)
Via della Domus Aurea
(Map 9 G1)
Ancient site

San Giovanni in
Laterano (p93)
Piazza di San Giovanni in
Laterano 4 (Map 9 H2)
Church

Santa Croce in
Gerusalemme (p93)
Piazza di Santa Croce in
Gerusalemme 12
(Map 10 B1)
Church

Santi Quattro Coronati (p87)
Via dei Santi Quattro Coronati
(Map 9 H1) 06 7047 5427
Church

Santo Stefano Rotondo (p87)
Via di Santo Stefano Rotondo
(Map 9 G2)
Church

Scala Santa (p91)
Piazza di San Giovanni in
Laterano (Map 10 A2)
Church

Teatro di Marcello (p87)
Via del Teatro di Marcello
(Map 9 D1)
Ancient site

Terme di Caracalla (p88)
Viale delle Terme di Caracalla
52 (Map 9 G3)
Ancient site

Ostiense & Garbatella

Centrale Montemartini (p92)
Via Ostiense 106 (Map 10 B4)
Gallery

San Paolo Fuori le Mura (p93)
Via Ostiense
(Ⓜ Basilica San Paolo)
Church

Southern Suburbs/
Appio Latino

Catacombe di San
Sebastiano (p95)
Via Appia Antica 136
(Bus Nos. 118, 218, 660)
Catacombs

San Sebastiano (p93)
Via Appia Antica 136
(Bus Nos. 118, 218, 660)
Church

Southern Suburbs/EUR

Museo della Civiltà
Romana (p89)
Piazza Giovanni Agnelli 10
(Ⓜ EUR Palasport; EUR Fermi)
Museum

Palazzo della Civiltà del
Lavoro (p91)
Viale della Civiltà del Lavoro
(Ⓜ EUR Palasport; EUR Fermi)
Fascist architecture

Southern Suburbs/
Ostia Antica

Ostia Antica (p95)
Viale dei Romagnoli 117
(Train to Ostia Antica)
Ancient site

Testaccio

Il Mattatoio (p83)
Piazza Orazio Giustiniani
(Map 5 G1)
Exhibition space

Performance

Ostiense & Garbatella

Acrobax Project (p99)
Via della Vasca Navale 6
(Ⓜ Basilica San Paolo)
06 558 2715
www.acrobax.org
Centro sociale

Classico Village (p105)
Via Giuseppe Libetta 3
(Map 10 C5)
Rock & pop venue

Teatro Palladium (p105)
Piazza Bartolomeo Romano 8
(Map 10 C5)
Multi-function venue

Southern Suburbs/EUR

Palacisalfa (p105)
Viale dell'Oceano
Atlantico 271d (Ⓜ EUR Fermi)
Rock & pop venue

Testaccio

Caffè Latino (p105)
Via di Monte Testaccio 96
(Map 8 D4)
Rock & pop venue

Spazio Boario-Villaggio
Globale (p104)
Lungotevere Testaccio-Ex
Mattatoio (Map 8 C4)
Centro sociale

Bars & Clubs

Capitolino & Palatino

Caffè Capitolino (p133)
Piazzale Caffarelli (Map 7 G5)
Bar

Celio & San Giovanni

Coming Out (p116)
Via San Giovanni in
Laterano 8 (Map 9 G1)
Club

Ostiense & Garbatella

Alpheus (p118)
Via del Commercio 36
(Map 10 C3)
Club

Distillerie Clandestine (p117)
Via Libetta 13 (Map 10 C5)
Bar

Ex Magazzini (p117)
Via dei Magazzini Generali 8b
(Map 10 B3)
Club

Goa (p118)
Via Libetta 13 (Map 10 C5)
Club

Southern Suburbs/
Prenestino Labicano

Circolo degli Artisti
(p119)
Via Casilinia Vecchia 42
(Map 10 D2)
Club

Testaccio

Akab (p116)
Via di Monte Testaccio 69
(Map 8 D4)
Club

Bar Zi Elena (p129)
Piazza Testaccio 42 (Map 8 D3)
Bar

Caruso Caffè de Oriente (p117)
Via di Monte Testaccio 36
(Map 8 C4)
Bar

Villa Farnesina (p93)
Via della Lungara 230
(Map 1 D5)
Villa

Trastevere

Santa Cecilia (p92)
Piazza Santa Cecilia
(Map 8 D2)
Church

San Francesco a Ripa (p78)
Piazza San Francesco
d'Assisi 88 (Map 8 C2)
Church

**Santa Maria in
Trastevere** (p92)
Piazza Santa Maria in
Trastevere (Map 8 C1)
Church

Tempietto del Bramante (p93)
Piazza San Pietro in Montorio
(Map 8 B1)
Church

Performance

Città del Vaticano & Prati

Alexanderplatz (p106)
Via Ostia 9 (Map 1 B2)
Jazz & blues venue

AS Roma Store (p101)
Piazza Colonna 360
(Map 7 F1)
06 678 6514
www.asromastore.it
Football goods store

Gianicolo

Teatro Ghione (p107)
Via delle Fornaci 37 (Map 1 C4)
Theatre

Trastevere

Big Mama (p107)
Vicolo San Francesco a Ripa 18
(Map 8 C2)
Jazz & blues venue

Lettere Caffè (p106)
Via San Francesco a Ripa
100–101 (Map 8 C2)
Literary venue

Nuovo Sacher (p106)
Largo Aschianghi 1 (Map 8 C2)
Cinema

Pasquino (p106)
Piazza Sant'Egidio 10
(Map 8 B1)
Cinema

Teatro Vascello (p107)
Via Giacinto Carini 78
(Map 8 A2)
Multi-function venue

Western Suburbs/
Gianicolense

Teatro India (p107)
Via L Pierantoni 6
(Map 8 C5)
Theatre

Bars & Clubs

Trastevere

Bar San Calisto (p119)
Piazza San Calisto 3–4
(Map 8 C1)
Bar

La Buca Di Bacco (p120)
Via San Francesco a Ripa 114
(Map 8 C1)
Bar

Friends Art Café (p119)
Piazza Trilussa 34
(Map 8 C1)
Bar

In Vino Veritas Art Bar (p120)
Via Garibaldi 2a
(Map 8 B1)
Bar

Molly Malone (p120)
Via dell'Arco di San Calisto 17
(Map 8 C1)
06 5833 0904
Pub

Ombre Rosse (p120)
Piazza Sant'Eguidio 12
(Map 8 B1)
Bar

Stardust (p120)
Vicolo dei Renzi 4
(Map 8 C1)
Bar

Western Suburbs/
Monte Mario

Bar-Ristorante Zodiaco (p135)
Viale del Parco Mellini 88–90
(Ⓜ Ottavanio, then bus 999)
Bar

Havens:
Parks & Gardens

Gianicolo

Orto Botanico (p135)
Largo Cristina di Svezia 24
(Map 8 B1)
Gardens

Parco del Gianicolo (p132)
(Map 1 C5)
Park

Trastevere

Villa Sciarra (p132)
(Map 8 A2)
Park

Western Suburbs/Aurelio

Villa Pamphili (p132)
(Train to San Pietro)
Park

Hotels

Città del Vaticano & Prati

Hotel Bramante (p148)   €€
Vicolo delle Palline 24
(Map 1 C3)

Hotel Colors (p149)   €
Via Boezio 31
(Map 1 D2)

Residenza Paolo VI (p149) €€
Via Paolo VI 29
(Map 1 C3)

Index by Type

Restaurants

Baked Goods

Fantasia del Pane (p34) €
Via Goito 9 (Map 5 G2)
East/Esquilino

Le Pain Quotidien (p37) €
Via Tomacelli 24–5 (Map 4 C3)
North/Tridente

Brunch

Ristorante Bramante (p39) €€
Via della Pace 25 (Map 6 C2)
06 6880 3916
Centre/Navona & Pantheon

East African

Africa (p40) €
Via Gaeta 26 (Map 5 G2)
East/Esquilino

Emilia-Romagnan

Colline Emiliane (p38) €€
Via degli Avignonesi 22
(Map 5 E3)
East/Quirinale & Monti

Enoteche

Il Bicchiere di Mastai (p31) €€€
Via dei Banchi Nuovi 52
(Map 6 B2)
Centre/Navona & Pantheon

Buccone (p65) €
Via di Ripetta 19–20
(Map 4 C2)
06 361 2154
North/Tridente

Casa Bleve (p30) €€
Via del Teatro Valle 48
(Map 6 E3)
Centre/Navona & Pantheon

Cavour 313 (p36) €
Via Cavour 313 (Map 5 E5)
06 678 5496
East/Quirinale & Monti

Città del Gusto (p45) €€
Via Enrico Fermi 161
Western Suburbs/Gianicolense

Costantini (p36) €
Piazza Cavour 16 (Map 5 E5)
06 321 3210
East/Quirinale & Monti

Cul de Sac (p36) €
Piazza Pasquino 73 (Map 6 D3)
06 880 1094
Centre/Navona & Pantheon

Enoteca Capranica (p36) €
Piazza Capranica 99 (Map 7 F2)
www.enotecacapranica.it
Centre/Navona & Pantheon

Enoteca Corsi (p32) €
Via del Gesù 87 (Map 7 F3)
Centre/Navona & Pantheon

Enoteca Ferrara (p71) €
Via del Moro 1a (Map 8 C1)
06 5833 3920
West/Trastevere

'Gusto (p35, p64) €€
Piazza Augusto Imperatore 9
(Map 4 C2)
North/Tridente

French

Le Bistrot d'Hubert (p36) €€
Via Sardegna 135 (Map 5 F1)
North/Pincio & Villa Borghese

Ice Cream

Giolitti (p30) €
Via Uffici Vicario 40 (Map 7 H1)
06 699 1243
Centre/Navona & Pantheon

Il Palazzo del Freddo di €
Giovanni Fassi (p30)
Via P Eugenio 65–7 (Map 5 H5)
06 446 4740
East/Esquilino

San Crispino (p30) €
Via Acaia 56 (Map 10 A4)
06 7045 0412
South/Celio & San Giovanni;
Via Panetteria 42 (Map 7 H1)
06 679 3924
East/Quirinale & Monti

International

Le Bain (p33) €€
Via delle Botteghe Oscure 32
(Map 7 F4)
Centre/Ghetto & Campo dei Fiori

Bloom (p30) €€
Via del Teatro Pace 30 (Map 6 C3)
Centre/Navona & Pantheon

Jazz Café (p29) €
Via Zanardelli 12 (Map 6 D2)
Centre/Navona & Pantheon

Mangiamoci (p34) €€
Salita di San Sebastianello
(Map 4 D2)
North/Pincio & Villa Borghese

La Pergola (p46) €€€
Hotel Cavalieri Hilton, Via
Cadlolo 101 (Ⓜ Ottaviano)
Western Suburbs/Monte Mario

Italian

Café Renault (p37) €
Via Nazionale 183b (Map 5 E4)
East/Quirinale & Monti

Città del Gusto (p45) €€
Via Enrico Fermi 161
Western Suburbs/Gianicolense

Il Convivio (p29) €€€
Vicolo dei Soldati (Map 6 D1)
Centre/Navona & Pantheon

Il Cortile (p44) €€
Via Alberto Mario 25 (Map 8 A3)
West/Trastevere

Da Fortunato (p31) €€€
Via del Pantheon 55
(Map 7 E2)
Centre/Navona & Pantheon

Da Settimio all'Arancio €€
(p37)
Via dell'Arancio 50 (Map 4 C3)
North/Tridente

Ditirambo (p28) €€
Piazza Cancelleria 75 (Map 6 D3)
Centre/Navona & Pantheon

'Gusto (p35) €€€
Piazza Augusto Imperatore 9
(Map 4 C2)
North/Tridente

Obikà (p31) €€
Via dei Prefetti 26a (Map 7 E1)
Centre/Navona & Pantheon

Ristorante Asinocotto (p44) €€
Via dei Vascellari (Map 8 D1)
West/Trastevere

Ristorante Trattoria (p29) €€€
Campo Marzio, Via del Pozzo
delle Cornacchie 25
(Map 7 E2)
Centre/Navona & Pantheon

Sette (p38, p146) €€€
Radisson SAS ES.Hotel, Via
Filippo Turati 171 (Map 5 H4)
East/Esquilino

La Tana dei Golosi (p40) €€€
Via di San Giovanni in
Laterano 220 (Map 9 H1)
South/Celio & San Giovanni

Tutti Frutti (p43) €
Via Luca della Robia 3a
(Map 8 D4)
South/Testaccio

Sora Lucia (p37) €
Via della Panetteria 41a
(Map 7 H1)
East/Quirinale & Monti

Japanese

Zen (p47) €€
Via degli Scipioni 243
(Map 1 C2)
West/Città del Vaticano & Prati

Mediterranean

Osteria dell'Ingegno €€
(p32)
Piazza di Pietra 45 (Map 7 F2)
Centre/Navona & Pantheon

Taverna Angelica (p47) €€
Via A Capponi 6 (Map 1 C3)
West/Città del Vaticano & Prati

Neapolitan

La Caffettiera (p31) €
Piazza di Pietra 65 (Map 7 F2)
Centre/Navona & Pantheon

Hostaria degli Artisti (p38) €
Via G Sommeiller 6 (Map 10 B1)
East/San Lorenzo

Pizza

Da Baffetto (p30) €
Via del Governo Vecchio 14
(Map 6 C3)
Centre/Navona & Pantheon

Da Vittorio (p44) €
Via di San Cosimato 14a
(Map 8 C1)
West/Trastevere

Est! Est!! Est!!! – €
Da Ricci (p39)
Via Genova 32 (Map 5 F4)
East/Quirinale & Monti

'Gusto (p35, p39, p64) €€
Piazza Augusto Imperatore 9
(Map 4 C2)
North/Tridente

Pizza Rè (p36) €
Via di Ripetta 14 (Map 4 C2)
North/Tridente

Pizzeria Dar Poeta (p47) €
Vicolo del Bologna 45
(Map 8 B1)
West/Trastevere

Pizzeria Remo
Testaccio (p43) €
Piazza Santa Maria
Liberatrice 44 (Map 8 C3)
South/Testaccio

Uffa Che Pizza (p38) €
Via dei Taurini 39
East/San Lorenzo

Roman

Agata e Romeo (p39) €€€
Via Carlo Alberto 45 (Map 5 G4)
East/Esquilino

Checchino dal 1887 (p41) €€
Via di Monte Testaccio 30
(Map 8 C4)
South/Testaccio

Da Bucatino (p43) €
Via Luca della Robia 84–6
(Map 8 D3)
South/Testaccio

Da Gino (p32) €
Vicolo Rosini 4 (Map 7 E1)
Centre/Navona & Pantheon

Domenico dal 1968 (p41) €€
Via Satrico 23 (Map 10 A4)
South/Celio & San Giovanni

The Kitchen (p44) €€
Via dei Conciatori 3 (Map 8 D4)
South/Testaccio

ReD (p126) €
Viale Pietro de Coubertin 30
(Map 2 D2) 06 8 069 1630
*Northern Suburbs/Flaminio &
Olimpico*

Sora Lella (p32) €€
Via di Ponte Quattro Capi 16,
Isola Tiberina (Map 8 D1)
Centre/Ghetto & Campo dei Fiori

Sora Margherita (p33) €
Piazza delle Cinque Scole 30
(Map 7 E5)
Centre/Ghetto & Campo dei Fiori

Trattoria Monti (p39) €€
Via San Vito 13 (Map 5 G5)
East/Esquilino

Trattoria Moschino (p129) €€
Piazza Brin 5 (Map 10 C5)
06 513 9473
South/Ostiense & Garbatella

Trattoria San Teodoro €€€
(p42)
Via dei Fienili 49–51 (Map 9 E1)
South/Capitolino & Palatino

Roman-Jewish

Al Pompiere (p33) €€
Palazzo Cenci, Via Santa Maria
dei Calderari 38 (Map 7 E5)
Centre/Ghetto & Campo dei Fiori

Piperno (p33) €€€
Via Monte dei Cenci 9
(Map 7 E5)
Centre/Ghetto & Campo dei Fiori

Zi Fenizia (p124) €
Via Santa Maria del Pianto
64–5 (Map 7 E5)
06 689 6976
Centre/Ghetto & Campo dei Fiori

Salads

Insalata Ricca (p28) €
Largo Chiavari (Map 6 D4)
Centre/Ghetto & Campo dei Fiori

Seafood

Al Presidente (p37) €€
Via in Arcione 95 (Map 7 H1)
East/Quirinale & Monti

F.I.S.H. (p40) €€
Via dei Serpenti 16 (Map 5 E5)
East/Quirinale & Monti

Riccioli Café (p31) €€€
Piazza Coppelle 10 (Map 7 E1)
Centre/Navona & Pantheon

Sicilian

Il Dito e la Luna (p41) €€
Via dei Sabelli 51
(Bus Nos. 204, 492)
East/San Lorenzo

Tuscan

Da Guido (p47) €
Via della Scala 31a (Map 8 B1)
West/Trastevere

Vegetarian

Arancia Blu (p40) €€
Via dei Latini 55–65 (Map 6 F4)
East/San Lorenzo

Il Margutta Ristorarte €€
(p34)
Via Margutta 118 (Map 4 C2)
North/Tridente

Vietnamese

Thien Kim (p28) €
Via Giulia 201 (Map 6 C5)
Centre/Ghetto & Campo dei Fiori

Shopping

Accessories

Bottega Veneta (p53)
Piazza San Lorenzo in Lucina
11–13 (Map 4 C3)
Centre/Navona & Pantheon

Buccellati (p63)
Via Condotti 31 (Map 4 D3)
North/Tridente

Bulgari (p62)
Via Condotti 10 (Map 4 D2)
North/Tridente

Cravatterie Nazionali (p63)
Via Vittoria 62 (Map 4 C2)
North/Tridente

Francesco Biasia (p66)
Via Due Macelli 62–62a
(Map 4 D3)
North/Tridente

Luisella Mariotti (p64)
Via di Gesù e Maria 20a
(Map 4 C2)
North/Tridente

Mandarina Duck (p61)
Via dei Due Macelli 59
(Map 4 D3)
North/Tridente

Modavì (p59)
Via di Campo Marzio 10c
(Map 7 E1)
Centre/Navona & Pantheon

Schostal (p64)
Via del Corso 158
(Map 4 C2)
North/Tridente

Beauty

Pro Fumum Durante (p60)
Via della Colonna Antonina 27
(Map 7 F2)
Centre/Navona & Pantheon

Books

Amore e Psiche (p70)
Via Santa Caterina da Siena 61
(Map 7 F3)
06 678 3908
Centre/Navona & Pantheon

Anglo-American Book Co (p70)
Via della Vite 102 (Map 4 D3)
06 679 5222
North/Tridente

Bibli (p71)
Via dei Fienaroli 28 (Map 8 C1)
West/Trastevere

La Diagonale (p70)
Via del Biscione 9a
(Map 6 D4)
06 6813 6812
Centre/Ghetto & Campo dei Fiori

Fahrenheit 451 (p70)
Piazza Campo dei Fiori 44
(Map 6 D4)
06 687 5930
Centre/Ghetto & Campo dei Fiori

Feltrinelli International (p70)
Via Vittorio Emanuele Orlando
78–81 (Map 5 F3) 06 487 0171
East/Esquilino

Libreria Francesco Ponti (p64)
Via Tomacelli 23 (Map 4 C3)
North/Tridente

Libreria dei Cinema (p70)
Via dei Fienaroli 31d (Map 8 C1)
06 581 7724
West/Trastevere

Index by Type

Shopping

Books *continued*

Libreria del Viaggiatore (p58)
Via del Pellegrino 78 (Map 6 B3)
Centre/Ghetto & Campo dei Fiori

Lion Bookshop (p70)
Via dei Greci 33–6 (Map 4 C2)
06 3265 4007
North/Tridente

Odradek (p70)
Via Banchi Vecchi 57 (Map 6 B3)
06 683 3451
www.odradek.it
Centre/Ghetto & Campo dei Fiori

Ta Matete (p70)
Via della Pilotta 16 (Map 4 D4)
06 679 1107
Centre/Navona & Pantheon

Children's Clothes

Rachele (p55)
Vicolo del Bollo 6–7 (Map 6 C4)
Centre/Ghetto & Campo dei Fiori

Concept Store

TAD (p62)
Via del Babuino 155a (Map 4 C2)
North/Tridente

Department Store

COIN (p65)
Piazzale Appio 7 (Map 10 A2)
06 708 0020
www.coin.it
South/Celio & San Giovanni

MAS (p65, p128)
Via dello Statuto 11 (Map 5 65)
06 446 8078
East/Esquilino

La Rinascente (p65)
Largo Chigi 20 (Map 7 G1)
06 679 7691
North/Tridente

Food & Drink

Antico Forno Roscioli (p59)
Via dei Giubbonari 21–2
(Map 6 D5)
Centre/Ghetto & Campo dei Fiori

Benedetto Franchi (p71)
Via Cola di Rienzo 200–204
(Map 4 A2)
West/Città del Vaticano & Prati

Biblioatea (p58)
Via dei Banchi Vecchi 124
(Map 6 B3)
Centre/Ghetto & Campo dei Fiori

Buccone (p65)
Via di Ripetta 19 (Map 4 C2)
North/Tridente

Emporio Libreria 'Gusto (p64)
Piazza A Imperatore 7 (Map 4 C2)
North/Tridente

Enoteca al Parlamento (p59)
Via dei Prefetti 15 (Map 7 E1)
Centre/Navona & Pantheon

**Enoteca di Sardegna
Pigna** (p60)
Via della Pigna 3a (Map 7 F3)
Centre/Navona & Pantheon

Enoteca Ferrara (p71)
Via del Moro 1 (Map 8 C1)
West/Trastevere

Forno di Campo dei Fiori (p57)
Piazza Campo dei Fiori 22
(Map 6 C4)
Centre/Ghetto & Campo dei Fiori

Panella, L'Arte del Pane (p69)
Largo Leopardi 2 (Map 5 G5)
East/Esquilino

**Pasticceria Ebraica "Il
Boccione"** (p58, p124)
Via Portico d'Ottavia 1
(Map 7 F5)
Centre/Ghetto & Campo dei Fiori

Trimani Enoteca (p68)
Via Goito 20 (Map 5 G2)
East/Esquilino

Volpetti (p70)
Via Marmorata 47 (Map 8 D3)
South/Aventino

International Designers

Alberta Ferretti (p61)
Via dei Condotti 34 (Map 4 C3)
06 699 1160
www.albertaferretti.com
North/Tridente

Armani (p61)
Via Condotti 77 (Map 4 C3)
06 699 1460
www.giorgioarmani.com
North/Tridente

D&G (p61)
Piazza di Spagna 93–6
(Map 4 D2)
06 6938 0870
www.dolcegabbana.it
North/Tridente

Dolce & Gabbana (p61)
Via Condotti 52
(Map 4 D2)
06 6938 0870
www.dolcegabbana.it
North/Tridente

Ermenegildo Zegna (p61)
Via Borgognona 7e (Map 4 C3)
06 678 9143
www.ermenegildozegna.it
North/Tridente

Fendi (p61)
Via Borgognona 36–40
(Map 4 C3)
06 696 661
www.fendi.it
North/Tridente

Ferragamo (p61)
Via Condotti 73–4 (Map 4 C3)
06 679 1565
www.ferragamo.com
North/Tridente

Frette (p61)
Piazza di Spagna 11
(Map 4 D2)
06 679 0673
www.frette.it
North/Tridente

Gucci (p61)
Via Borgognona 7d (Map 4 C3)
Via Condotti 68a
(Map 4 C3)
Via Condotti 8 (Map 4 C3)
06 679 0405
www.gucci.com
North/Tridente

Mariella Burani (p61)
Via Bocca di Leone 28
(Map 4 C2)
06 679 0630
www.mariellaburani.it
North/Tridente

Missoni (p61)
Piazza di Spagna 78
(Map 4 D2)
06 679 2555
www.missoni.it
North/Tridente

Moschino (p61)
Via Borgognona 32a (Map 4 C3)
www.moschino.it
North/Tridente

Prada (p61)
Via Condotti 91 (Map 4 C3)
06 679 4879
www.prada.com
North/Tridente

Sergio Rossi (p61)
Piazza di Spagna 97–100
(Map 4 D2)
06 678 3245
www.sergiorossi.com
North/Tridente

Valentino (p61)
Via del Babuino 61 (Map 4 C2)
06 3600 1930
Via Condotti 13 (Map 4 C3)
06 6920 0618
Via Bocca di Leone 15–16
(Map 4 C2)
06 6920 09 06
www.valentino.it
North/Tridente

Versace (p61)
Via Borgognona 24–5
(Map 4 C3)
06 679 5037
Via Bocca di Leone 26–7
(Map 4 C2)
06 678 0521
www.versace.com
North/Tridente

High-Street Fashion

Avant (p65)
Via del Corso 177 (Map 4 C2)
06 228 0104
North/Tridente

Benetton (p65)
Via del Corso 422–3 (Map 4 D2)
06 6810 2520
www.benetton.com
North/Tridente

Brooks (p65)
Via Tarvisio 4 (Ⓜ Bologna)
06 841 3653
Northern Suburbs/Trieste

For the very latest on Rome go to ≫ www.realcity.dk.com

Sisley (p65)
Via del Corso 413–15 (Map 4 D2)
Via Condotti 59 (Map 4 C3)
www.sisley.com
North/Tridente

Sportstaff (p65)
Piazza di Spagna 84 (Map 4 D2)
06 678 1599
North/Tridente

Stefanel (p65)
Via Frattina 31–2
(Map 4 D3) 06 6792 6676
Via del Corso 123 (Map 4 C3)
06 6992 5783 www.stefanel.it
North/Tridente

Interiors

Giorgi & Febbi (p57)
Piazza della Rotonda 61–2
(Map 7 E2)
Centre/Navona & Pantheon

GiuncArt (p58)
Via del Pellegrino 93
(Map 6 C3)
Centre/Ghetto & Campo dei Fiori

Modigliani (p61)
Via Condotti 24 (Map 4 D2)
North/Tridente

Lingerie

La Perla (p65)
Via Condotti 79 (Map 4 D2)
North/Tridente

Simona (p63)
Via del Corso 82–3 (Map 4 C2)
North/Tridente

Yamamay (p64)
Via Frattina 86 (Map 4 C3)
North/Tridente

Markets

**Campo dei Fiori Produce
Market** (p125) (Map 6 D4)
Centre/Ghetto & Campo dei Fiori

**Piazza dell'Unità Produce
Market** (p67)
(Map 1 C2)
West/Città del Vaticano & Prati

**Piazza San Cosimato Produce
Market** (p67)
(Map 8 C2)
West/Trastevere

**Porta Portese Flea
Market** (p125)
Via Portuense
(Map 8 B5)
West/Trastevere

**Testaccio Produce
Market** (p129)
(Map 8 D3)
South/Testaccio

Via Sannio Flea Market (p124)
San Giovanni
(Map 10 A2)
South/Celio & San Giovanni

Men's Clothes

Amomamma (p54)
Via dei Giubbonari 49
(Map 6 D4)
Centre/Ghetto & Campo dei Fiori

**Il Discount dell'Alta
Moda** (p66)
Via di Gesù e Maria 14–16a
(Map 4 C2)
North/Tridente

empresa (p54)
Via del Giubbonari 25–6
(Map 6 D4)
Centre/Ghetto & Campo dei Fiori

Prototype (p54)
Via dei Giubbonari 50
(Map 6 D4)
Centre/Ghetto & Campo dei Fiori

SBU (p53)
Via di S Pantaleo 68
(Map 6 D3)
Centre/Navona & Pantheon

Music

Disfunzioni Musicali (p69)
Via degli Etruschi 4
(Tram to Lodi)
East/San Lorenzo

Goodfellas (p69)
Circonvallazione Casilina 44
(Tram to Lodi)
Eastern Suburbs/Prenestino

Soul Food (p68)
Via di San Giovanni in
Laterano 192–4
(Map 9 H1)
South/Celio & San Giovanni

One-Offs

Alinari (p65)
Via Alibert 16a (Map 4 D2)
North/Tridente

Brocante (p60)
Via dei Pastini 15–16
(Map 7 F2)
*Centre/Ghetto & Campo
dei Fiori*

Campo Marzio Design (p57)
Via di Campo Marzio 41
(Map 4 C3)
Centre/Navona & Pantheon

Ferrari Store (p53)
Via Tomacelli 147 (Map 4 C3)
Centre/Navona & Pantheon

Galleria d'Arte Sacra (p57)
Via dei Cestari 15 (Map 7 E3)
Centre/Navona & Pantheon

Marmi Line (p52)
Via dei Coronari 141–5
(Map 6 C2)
Centre/Navona & Pantheon

Nostalgica (p63)
Via di Ripetta 30–31 (Map 4 C2)
North/Tridente

Officina della Carta (p70)
Via Benedetta 26b (Map 8 C1)
West/Trastevere

La Vetrata di Passagrilli (p68)
Via del Boschetto 94
(Map 5 E5)
East/Quirinale & Monti

Shoes

AVC by Adriana Campanile
(p62)
Piazza di Spagna 88 (Map 4 D2)
North/Tridente

Borini (p55)
Via dei Pettinari 86–7
(Map 6 D5)
Centre/Ghetto & Campo dei Fiori

Elisheva (p55)
Via dei Baullari 19 (Map 6 C4)
Centre/Ghetto & Campo dei Fiori

Fausto Santini (p62)
Via Frattina 120
(Map 4 D3)
North/Pincio & Villa Borghese

Joseph Debach (p71)
Vicolo del Cinque 19 (Map 8 C1)
West/Trastevere

NuYorica (p54)
Piazza Pollarola 36–7
(Map 6 D4)
Centre/Ghetto & Campo dei Fiori

Vintage &
Secondhand

Le Gallinelle (p67)
Via del Boschetto 76
(Map 5 E4)
East/Quirinale & Monti

Maurizio de Nisi (p68)
Via Panisperna 51 (Map 5 E4)
East/Quirinale & Monti

Michel Harem (p61)
Via Sistina 137a (Map 5 E3)
North/Pincio & Villa Borghese

People (p55)
Piazza del Teatro Pompeo 4a
(Map 6 D4)
Centre/Ghetto & Campo dei Fiori

Pinko (p53)
Via dei Giubbonari 76–7
(Map 6 D4)
Centre/Ghetto & Campo dei Fiori

Pulp (p67)
Via del Boschetto 140 (Map 5 E5)
East/Quirinale & Monti

Retrò (p56)
Piazza del Fico 20–21 (Map 6 C2)
Centre/Navona & Pantheon

Women's Clothes

Abitart (p66)
Via della Croce 46–7
(Map 4 C2)
North/Tridente

Angelo di Nepi (p57)
Via dei Giubbonari 28
(Map 6 D5)
Centre/Ghetto & Campo dei Fiori

Arsenale (p52)
Via del Governo Vecchio 64
(Map 6 C3)
Centre/Navona & Pantheon

Campo de' Fiori 52 (p54)
Piazza del Paradiso 72
(Map 6 D4)
Centre/Ghetto & Campo dei Fiori

Santa Maria del Popolo (p82)
Piazza del Popolo 12 (Map 4 C1)
North/Tridente

Santa Maria in Cosmedin (p90)
Piazza della Bocca della Verità
(Map 9 A1)
South/Capitolino & Palatino

Santa Maria in Montesanto (p82)
Piazza del Popolo (Map 4 C1)
North/Tridente

Santa Maria in Trastevere (p92)
Piazza Santa Maria in
Trastevere (Map 8 C1)
West/Trastevere

Santa Maria Maggiore (p93)
Piazza di Santa Maria
Maggiore (Map 5 G4)
06 483 195
East/Esquilino

Santa Maria Sopra Minerva (p77)
Piazza della Minerva (Map 7 F3)
Centre/Navona & Pantheon

San Paolo Fuori le Mura (p93)
Via Ostiense
(Ⓜ Basilica San Paolo)
06 541 0341
South/Ostiense & Garbatella

St Peter's Basilica (p12, p94)
(Map 1 B3)
West/Città del Vaticano & Prati

San Pietro in Vincoli (p90, p91)
Piazza di San Pietro in Vincoli
(Map 5 F5)
06 488 2865
East/Esquilino

Santi Quattro Coronati (p87)
Via dei Santi Quattro Coronati
(Map 9 G1)
06 7047 5427
South/Celio & San Giovanni

Santa Sabina (p91)
Via Santa Sabina (Map 8 D2)
South/Aventino

San Sebastiano (p93)
Via Appia Antica 136
(Bus Nos. 118, 218, 660)
06 780 8847
Southern Suburbs/Appio Latina

San Silvestro in Capite (p91)
Piazza San Silvestro
(Map 4 D3)
North/Tridente

Santo Stefano Rotondo (p87)
Via di Santo Stefano Rotondo
(Map 9 G2)
06 7049 3717
South/Celio & San Giovanni

Scala Santa (p91)
Piazza di San Giovanni in
Laterano (Map 10 A2)
06 772 6641
South/Celio & San Giovanni

Trinità dei Monti (p81)
Piazza della Trinita dei Monti
(Map 4 D2)
North/Pincio & Villa Borghese

Fountains

Fontana della Barcaccia (p81)
Piazza di Spagna (Map 4 D2)
North/Tridente

Fontana delle Api (p84)
Piazza Barberini (Map 5 E3)
North/Pincio & Villa Borghese

Fontana di Trevi (p15, p86)
(Map 7 G1)
East/Quirinale & Monti

Quattro Fiumi (p86)
Piazza Navona (Map 6 D2)
Centre/Navona & Pantheon

Tartarughe (p86)
Piazza Mattei (Map 7 E5)
Centre/Ghetto & Campo dei Fiori

Il Tritone (p84)
Piazza Barberini (Map 5 E3)
North/Pincio & Villa Borghese

Galleries & Exhibition Spaces

Académie Francaise (p85)
Villa Medici, Viale Trinita dei
Monti 1a (Map 4 D2)
06 6992 1653
North/Tridente

British School (p85)
Via Gramsci 61 (Map 2 D4)
06 326 4931
www.bsr.ac.uk
Northern Suburbs/Flaminio & Olimpico

Centrale Montemartini (p92)
Via Ostiense 106 (Map 10 B4)
South/Ostiense & Garbatella

Galleria Borghese
(p13, p77, p79, p84)
Villa Borghese (Map 3 F5)
North/Pincio & Villa Borghese

Galleria Doria Pamphilj
(p77, p78)
Palazzo Doria, Piazza del
Collegio Romano 2 (Map 7 G3)
Centre/Navona & Pantheon

Galleria Nazionale d'Arte Antica (p84, p173)
Palazzo Barberini, Piazza
Barberini (Map 5 E3)
North/Pincio & Villa Borghese

Galleria Nazionale d'Arte Moderna (p85, p173)
Viale delle Belle Arti 131
(Map 3 E5)
06 322 981
www.gnam.arti.beniculturali.it
North/Pincio & Villa Borghese

Galleria Spada (p79)
Palazzo Spada, Piazza
Capo di Ferro (Map 6 D5)
Centre/Ghetto & Campo dei Fiori

MACRO (p83)
Via Reggio Emilia 54
(Map 5 G1)
North/Pincio & Villa Borghese

Il Mattatoio (p83)
Piazza Orazio Giustiniani
(Map 5 G1)
South/Testaccio

MAXXI (p83)
Via Guido Reni 10 (Map 2 B2)
Northern Suburbs/Flaminio & Olimpico

Scuderie del Quirinale (p85)
Via XXIV Maggio 16
(Map 5 E4)
East/Quirinale & Monti

Monuments

Ara Pacis (p81)
Via di Ripetta, Lungotevere in
Augusta (Map 4 C2)
North/Tridente

Column of Marcus Aurelius (p80)
Piazza Colonna
(Map 7 F1)
Centre/Navona & Pantheon

Museums

Keats-Shelley Memorial House (p81)
Piazza di Spagna 26
(Map 4 D2)
North/Pincio & Villa Borghese

Musei Capitolini (p14, p88)
Piazza Campidoglio
(Map 7 G5)
South/Capitolino & Palatino

Museo Crypta Balbi (p78)
Via delle Botteghe Oscure 31
(Map 7 F4)
Centre/Ghetto & Campo dei Fiori

Museo d'Arte Ebraica (p124)
Lungotevere dei Cenci
(Map 8 D1)
06 6840 0661
Centre/Ghetto & Campo dei Fiori

Museo della Civiltà Romana (p91)
Piazza Giovanni Agnelli 10
(Ⓜ EUR Palasport; EUR Fermi)
Southern Suburbs/EUR

Museo di Roma (p77)
Palazzo Braschi, Via di San
Pantaleo 10 (Map 6 D3)
Centre/Navona & Pantheon

Museo Hendrik Christian Anderson (p83)
Via Pasquale Stanislao
Mancini 20
(Map 4 B1)
North/Pincio & Villa Borghese

Museo Nazionale di Villa Giulia (p127)
Piazzale Villa Giulia 9
(Map 2 D5)
06 322 6571
North/Pincio & Villa Borghese

Museo Nazionale Romano (p86)
Palazzo Massimo alle Terme:
Largo di Villa Peretti 1 (Map 5 G3)
Aula Ottagonale: Via Parigi
(Map 5 G3)
Terme di Diocleziano: Via dei
Nicola (Map 5 G3)
East/Esquilino

Index by Type

Art & Architecture

Museums *continued*

Palazzo Altemps (p76)
Piazza Sant'Apollinare 48
(Map 6 D1)
Centre/Navona & Pantheon

Palazzo Barberini (p84)
Piazza Barberini (Map 5 E3)
North/Pincio & Villa Borghese

Palazzo Corsini (p93)
Via della Lungara 10 (Map 1 D5)
West/Gianicolo

Vatican Museums (p13, p94)
(Map 1 B3)
West/Città del Vaticano & Prati

One-Offs

Catacombe di San Sebastiano (p91, p95)
Via Appia Antica 136
(Bus Nos. 118, 218)
Southern Suburbs/Appio Latino

Palazzo della Civiltà del Lavoro (p91)
Viale della Civiltà del Lavoro
(Ⓜ EUR Palasport; EUR Fermi)
Southern Suburbs/EUR

Piazza dei Cavalieri di Malta (p90)
(Map 8 D3)
South/Aventino

Ponte Sant'Angelo (p78)
(Map 6 B1)
Centre/Ghetto & Campo dei Fiori

Spanish Steps (p15, p81)
(Map 4 D2)
North/Pincio & Villa Borghese

Tempietto del Bramante (p93)
Piazza San Pietro in Montorio
(Map 8 B1)
West/Trastevere

Palaces & Villas

Palazzo Chigi (p80)
Piazza Colonna
(Map 7 F1)
Centre/Navona & Pantheon

Palazzo del Quirinale (p85)
Piazza Monte Cavallo
(Map 5 E4)
East/Quirinale & Monti

Palazzo Farnese (p90)
Piazza Farnese (Map 6 C4)
Centre/Ghetto & Campo dei Fiori

Villa Farnesina (p93)
Via della Lungara 230
(Map 1 D5)
West/Gianicolo

Squares

Campidoglio (p88)
Piazza Campidoglio
(Map 7 G5)
South/Capitolino & Palatino

Piazza Barberini (p84)
(Map 5 E3)
North/Pincio & Villa Borghese

Piazza della Bocca della Verità (p90) (Map 9 E1)
South/Capitolino & Palatino

Piazza del Popolo (p82)
(Map 4 C1)
North/Tridente

Piazza di Spagna (p81)
(Map 4 D2)
North/Tridente

Synagogue

Synagogue (p124)
Lungotevere Cenci
(Map 8 D1)
Centre/Ghetto & Campo dei Fiori

Performance

Centri Sociali

Acrobat Project (p99)
Via della Vasca Navale 6
(Ⓜ Basilica San Paolo)
06 9761 6630
www.acrobax.org
Ostiense & Garbatella

Brancaleone (p121)
Via Levana 11
(Train to Nomentana)
Northern Suburbs/Montesacro

Forte Prenestino (p99)
Via Federico Delpino
(Train to Centocelle)
06 2180 7855
Eastern Suburbs/Centocelle

Rialto Sant'Ambrogio (p132)
Via Sant'Ambrogio 4
(Map 7 F5)
Centre/Ghetto & Campo dei Fiori

Spazio Boario-Villaggio Globale (p104)
Lungotevere Testaccio
(Map 8 C4)
South/Testaccio

Cinema

Cinema Teatro-Farnese (p101)
Piazza Campo dei Fiori 56
(Map 6 D4)
Centre/Ghetto & Campo dei Fiori

Filmstudio (p105)
Via degli Orti d'Alibert 1c
(Map 1 D5)
West/Gianicolo

Nuovo Sacher (p106)
Largo Aschianghi 1
(Map 8 C2)
West/Trastevere

Comedy

Teatro Ambra Jovinelli (p102)
Via G Pepe 43–7
(Map 5 H5)
East/Esquilino

Jazz & Blues Venues

Alexanderplatz (p106)
Via Ostia 9
(Map 1 B2)
West/Città del Vaticano & Prati

Big Mama (p107)
Vicolo San Francesco a Ripa 18
(Map 8 C2)
West/Trastevere

Casa del Jazz (p103)
Viale di Porta Ardeatina 55
(Map 9 G5)
South/San Giovanni

Modo (p100)
Vicolo del Fico 3
(Map 6 C2)
Centre/Navona & Pantheon

Literary Venue

Lettere Caffè (p106)
Via San Francesco a Ripa 100–101 (Map 8 C2)
West/Trastevere

Multi-Function Venues

Auditorium Parco della Musica (p102, p126)
Via Pietro de Coubertin 15
(Map 2 C2)
Northern Suburbs/Flaminio & Olimpico

Il Posto delle Fragole (p103)
Via Carlo Botta 51
(Map 9 H1)
East/Esquilino

Teatro Argentina (p100)
Largo Argentina 52 (Map 7 E4)
Centre/Ghetto & Campo dei Fiori

Teatro Palladium (p105)
Piazza Bartolomeo Romano 8
(Map 10 C5)
South/Ostiense & Garbatella

Teatro Vascello (p107)
Via Giacinto Carini 78
(Map 8 A2)
West/Trastevere

Opera

Teatro dell'Opera di Roma (p101)
Piazza Beniamino Gigli 1
(Map 5 F3)
East/Esquilino

Rock & Pop Venues

Caffè Latino (p105)
Via di Monte Testaccio 96
(Map 8 D4)
South/Testaccio

Classico Village (p105)
Via Giuseppe Libetta 3
(Map 10 C5)
South/Ostiense & Garbatella

Locanda Atlantide (p103)
Via dei Lucani 22b
(Tram lines 3, 19)
East/San Lorenzo

Palacisalfa (p105)
Viale dell'Oceano Atlantico
271d (Ⓜ EUR Fermi)
Southern Suburbs/EUR

La Palma (p103)
Via Giuseppe Mirri 35
(Ⓜ Tiburtina)
Eastern Suburbs/Portonaccio

Sports Stadiums

Stadio Flaminio (p101)
Viale Tiziano
(Map 2 A1)
*Northern Suburbs/Flaminio &
Olimpico*

Stadio Olimpico (p101)
Viale dello Stadio Olimpico
(Ⓜ Flaminia, then bus No. 225)
*Northern Suburbs/Flaminio &
Olimpico*

Theatre

Teatro Ghione (p107)
Via delle Fornaci 37
(Map 1 C4)
West/Gianicolo

Teatro India (p107)
Via L Pierantoni 6
(Map 8 C5)
*Western Suburbs/
Gianicolense*

Teatro Valle (p101)
Via del Teatro Valle 21
(Map 7 E3)
Centre/Navona & Pantheon

Ticket Outlets

Orbis (p107)
Piazza Esquilino 37
(Map 5 F4)
06 482 7403
East/Esqulino

Ricordi (p107)
Via del Corso 56
(Map 4 C2)
06 361 2370
Centre/Navona & Pantheon

Hotels

Cheap

**Albergo del Sole al
Biscione** (p140)
Via del Biscione 76 (Map 6 D4)
Centre/Ghetto & Campo dei Fiori

Antica Locanda (p145)
Via del Boschetto 84
(Map 5 E4)
East/Quirinale & Monti

B&B Vacanze Romane (p144)
Via Carlo Alberto 26
(Map 5 G4)
East/Esquilino

Casa di Santa Brigida (p143)
Piazza Farnese 96 (Map 6 C4)
06 6889 2596
Centre/Ghetto & Campo dei Fiori

Casa Smith (p148)
Piazza I Nievo 1 (Map 8 B3)
West/Trastevere

**Franciscan Sisters of
Atonement** (p143)
Via Monte Gallo 105 (Map 1 B5)
06 630 782 (Curfew 11pm)
West/Gianicolo

Hostel des Artistes (p138)
Via Villafranca 20 (Map 5 H2)
East/Esquilino

Hotel Colors (p144)
Via Boezio 31 (Map 1 D2)
West/Città del Vaticano & Prati

Hotel Navona (p140)
Via dei Sediari 8 (Map 7 E3)
Centre/Navona & Pantheon

Hotel Parlamento (p144)
Via delle Convertite 5 (Map 7 F1)
North/Tridente

Hotel Santa Prisca (p148)
Largo M Gelsomini 25
(Map 8 D4)
South/Aventino

**Nostra Signora di
Lourdes** (p143)
Via Sistina 113 (Map 5 E3)
06 474 5324 (Curfew 10:30pm)
North/Pincio & Villa Borghese

Pantheon View B&B (p140)
Via del Seminario 87
(Map 7 F2)
Centre/Navona & Pantheon

Pensione Panda (p143)
Via della Croce 35
(Map 4 C2)
North/Tridente

Moderate

Casa di Carlo IV (p140)
Via dei Banchi Vecchi 132
(Map 6 B2)
Centre/Ghetto & Campo dei Fiori

Casa Howard (p142)
Via Capo le Case 18 (Map 4 D3)
North/Tridente

Hotel Abitart (p147)
Via Matteucci 10–20
(Map 10 C3)
South/Ostiense & Garbatella

Hotel Aleph (p143)
Via di San Basilio 15
(Map 5 E2)
North/Pincio & Villa Borghese

Hotel Aventino (p148)
Via San Domenico 10
(Map 8 D3)
South/Aventino

Hotel Bramante (p148)
Vicolo delle Palline 24
(Map 1 C3)
West/Città del Vaticano & Prati

L'Hotel Cinquantatrè (p142)
Via di San Basilio 53
(Map 5 E3)
North/Pincio & Villa Borghese

Hotel dei Gladiatori (p145)
Via Labicana 125 (Map 9 G1)
East/Esquilino

Hotel Lancelot (p147)
Via Capo d'Africa 47
(Map 9 G1)
South/Celio & San Giovanni

Hotel Locarno (p144)
Via della Penna 22 (Map 4 B2)
North/Tridente

Hotel Piemonte (p145)
Via Vicenza 34a (Map 5 G3)
East/Esquilino

Hotel dei Portoghesi (p140)
Via dei Portoghesi 1 (Map 6 D1)
Centre/Navona & Pantheon

**Hotel Santa Maria in
Trastevere** (p149)
Vicolo del Piede 2 (Map 8 C1)
West/Trastevere

Hotel Villa delle Rose (p145)
Via Vicenza 5 (Map 5 G3)
East/Esquilino

Locanda Cairoli (p141)
Piazza Benedetto Cairoli 2
(Map 7 E5)
Centre/Ghetto & Campo dei Fiori

Residenza Frattina (p143)
Via Frattina 104 (Map 4 D3)
North/Tridente

Residenza Monti (p145)
Via dei Serpenti 15 (Map 5 E5)
East/Quirinale & Monti

Residenza Paolo VI (p149)
Via Paolo VI 29 (Map 1 C3)
West/Città del Vaticano & Prati

Expensive

Forty Seven (p147)
Via Petroselli 47
(Map 9 E1)
South/Capitolino & Palatino

Hotel Art (p141)
Via Margutta 56 (Map 4 C2)
North/Tridente

Hotel Capo d'Africa (p147)
Via Capo d'Africa 54
(Map 9 G1)
South/Celio & San Giovanni

Hotel Eden (p142)
Via Ludovisi 49 (Map 4 D2)
North/Pincio & Villa Borghese

Hotel Exedra (p147)
Piazza della Repubblica 147
(Map 5 F3)
East/Esquilino

Hotel de Russie (p133, p142)
Via del Babuino 9
(Map 4 C1)
North/Tridente

Radisson SAS ES.Hotel (p146)
Via Filippo Turati 171 (Map 5 H5)
East/Esquilino

General Index

General Index

General Index

Acknowledgments

Produced by Departure Lounge LLP

Editorial Director Naomi Peck

Art Director Lisa Kosky

Project Editor Clare Tomlinson

Designer Bernhard Wölf

Assistant Editor Debbie Woska

Design and editoral assistance Julius Honnor and Lee Redmond

Researchers Daniela Ripoli, Rita Selvaggio and Giovanni Martucci-Evans

Proofreaders Sylvia Tombesi-Walton and Gary Werner

Indexer Hilary Bird

Published by DK

Publishing Managers Jane Ewart and Scarlett O'Hara

Senior Editor Christine Stroyan

Senior Designers Paul Jackson and Marisa Renzullo

Website Editor Gouri Banerji

Cartographic Editor Casper Morris

DTP Designers Jason Little and Natasha Lu

Production Coordinator Shane Higgins

Fact Checker Gerard Hutchings

PHOTOGRAPHY PERMISSIONS

The publishers would like to thank all the churches, museums, hotels, restaurants, bars, clubs, shops, galleries and other sights for their assistance and kind permission to photograph at their establishments.

Placement key: tc = top centre; tl = top left; tr = top right; cl = centre left; cla = centre left above; cr = centre right; crc = centre right centre; crb = centre right below; b = bottom; bl = bottom left; br = bottom right.

The publishers would like to thank the following companies and picture libraries for permission to reproduce their photographs:

ALAMY IMAGES: AA World Travel Library 6–7; Image State/Pictor International 1; CASA HOWARD: 139tc, 139tr, 142cl; CITTÀ DEL GUSTO: 45b; FAUSTO SANTINI: 62tl; FERRARI STORE: 53cl; FORTY SEVEN: 147cla; GOA: 111cl; HOTEL ALEPH: 138tl, 143tr; HOTEL ART: 141tr; HOTEL CAPO D'AFRICA: 147cr; HOTEL EDEN: 139tl, 142tr; HOTEL DEI PORTOGHESI: 140crb; HOTEL DE RUSSIE: 133tr; 142cr; HOTEL SANTA MARIA TRASTEVERE: 138bl, 149tl; LIBRERIA DEL CINEMA: 70bl; MODO: 100tl; LA NOTTE BIANCA: 19tr; OBIKÀ: 31tr; LA PERGOLA: 27cr, 46cla, 46cr, 46b; PISCINA DELL'HOTEL PARCO DEI PRINCIPI: 133cr; RADISSON SAS ES Hotel: 38tl, 116tl, 146cla, 146bl, 146br; RISTORANTE TRATTORIA: 29br; TEATRO VALLE: 101cla; VILLA ADA: 17tl; www.2night.it: 120cl.

Full Page Picture Captions: The Colosseum: 8–9; Casa Bleve: 24–5; Abitart: 48–9; Musei Capitolini: 72–3; Teatro Argentina: 90–91; Supperclub: 108–9; Campo de Fiori: 122–3; Giardino degli Aranci: 130–31; Hotel Locarno: 136–7.

Jacket Images

Front and Spine: ALAMY IMAGES: Image State/Pictor International.

Back: DK IMAGES: all.

Rome Transport Map

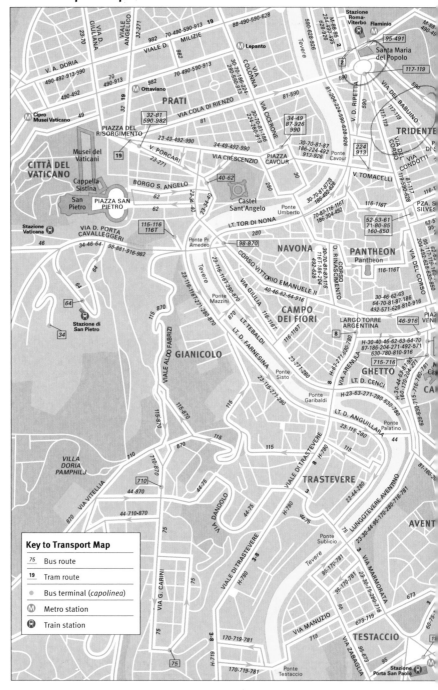

Key to Transport Map

75	Bus route
19	Tram route
●	Bus terminal (*capolinea*)
Ⓜ	Metro station
🚆	Train station